CAMBRIDGE AND ITS COLLEGES

CAMBRIDGE AND ITS COLLEGES

ALEXANDER HAMILTON THOMPSON

9 789356 145856
ISBN: 978-93-5614-585-6

Published: 1899

LECTOR HOUSE

LECTOR HOUSE LLP
E-MAIL: info@lectorhouse.com

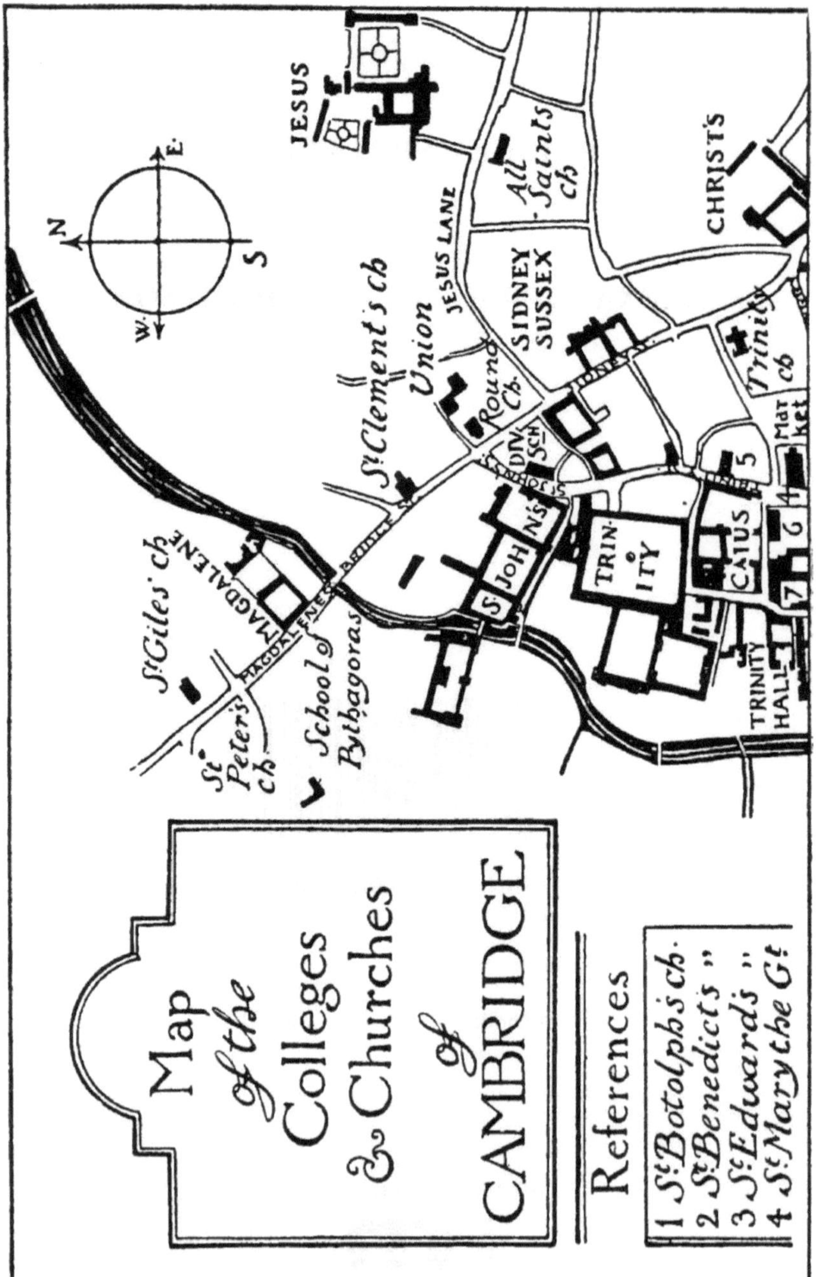

Map of the Colleges & Churches of Cambridge

References

1 *S*[t]. *Botolph's ch.* 2 *S*[t]. *Benedict's ch.* 3 *S*[t]. *Edward's ch.*

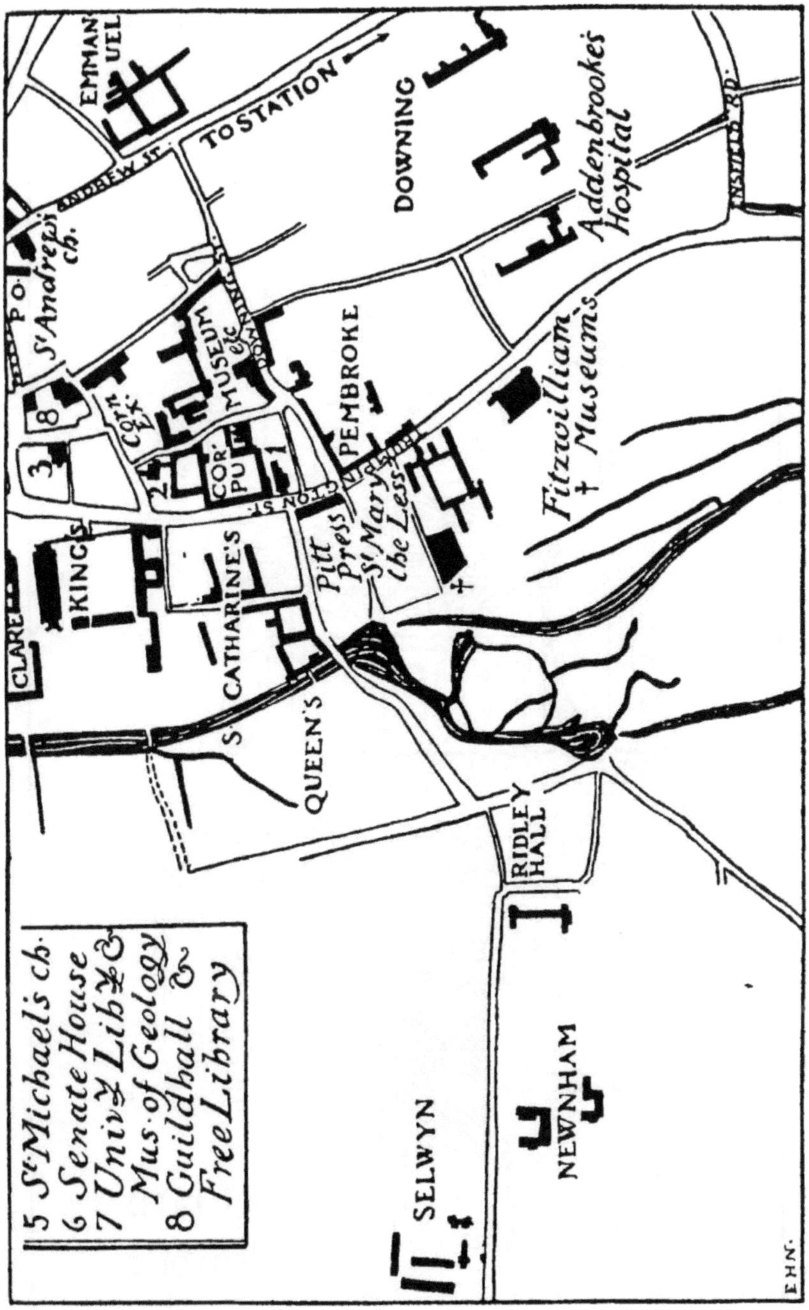

4 *S^{t}. Mary the G^{t}.* 5 *S^{t}. Michael's ch.* 6 *Senate House*

7 *Univ^{y}. Lib^{y}. & Mus. of Geology* 8 *Guildhall & Free Library*

The Gate of Honour, Caius College

CAMBRIDGE AND ITS COLLEGES

BY

A· HAMILTON · THOMPSON · B.A.

St John's College

ILLUSTRATED BY
EDMVND · H · NEW

"Ground where the grass had yielded to the steps
Of generations of illustrious men."

1899

TO
MY MOTHER

PREFACE

So much has been written about Cambridge that it is difficult to say anything new; and this little book is therefore merely an attempt to put together recorded facts in an orderly way. I have followed throughout the arrangement adopted by Mr Wells in his book on "Oxford and its Colleges," and have also borrowed his method of marking the portraits of college worthies with an asterisk. Every writer on Cambridge must be under a great obligation to Willis and Clark's Architectural History of the University; and Mr Atkinson's lately published book gives a singular completeness to the authorities for the architectural side of the question. Building at Cambridge, however, is a complex problem,—the history of Clare and the University Church are cases in point—and to follow out carefully every date and mark every alteration would be beyond these limits. My endeavour has been, therefore, to indicate the general date of every building rather than to assign a date to every particular part of its construction. For the historical part of the book, the authorities, grave and anecdotal, are too numerous to mention. Among modern works on the subject, I owe a great deal to Mr J. W. Clark's "Cambridge: Historical and Picturesque Notes" (Seeley, 1890). I am sure, too, that whatever interest my own part in this book may lack, Mr New's drawings will more than supply.

WISBECH,
April 23, 1898.

CONTENTS

LIST OF ILLUSTRATIONS

NOTE

The drawings have been made from photographs mostly taken by Messrs Stearn of Cambridge and Messrs Valentine.

CHAPTER I

CAMBRIDGE

Dr Caius' ingenious contention that Cambridge was founded in 3538 B.C. by Cantaber, a Spanish prince, has never received the support which its audacity deserves. The town cannot pretend to so great an antiquity, nor is its Roman origin even certain. It stood in the middle of a country intersected by Roman lines of road; in no part of England are Roman and British remains more plentiful and more interesting. The Via Devana, the great highroad from Colchester to Chester, was the road which runs through the modern town from the station to Magdalene Bridge, and continues in a straight line to Godmanchester and Huntingdon. The Via Iceniana, or Icknield Way, which ran straight across England from the Eastern Counties, parts company with the Cambridge road on Newmarket Heath, and pursues an undulating course south-westward to Royston and Hitchin. Ermine Street, the Old North Road, ran through Caxton, ten miles west of Cambridge, and met the Via Devana at Huntingdon. At Gogmagog Hills, five miles out of the town, we can trace the remains of Vandlebury Camp, which commanded the course of the Roman roads, and looked over the southern Fens and the Essex border. The familiar name of Grantchester is certainly of Roman origin. Instances might be multiplied to show how important this country was to Roman strategy. But there is no direct evidence to prove that Cambridge of to-day represents the ancient Camboritum. The Castle Hill, that odd mound from which so good a view of the town is obtained, is supposed to be in its origin Saxon; it formed an important outpost against the Danes, who have left so many traces of their occupation in Norfolk and Suffolk. And the municipal history of Cambridge certainly begins with Saxon times, and it was the seat of one of the earliest Gilds. Mr Atkinson, who has so admirably traced the municipal constitution of the town, gives us some details of the purpose and form of the Cambridge Gild of Thanes. It was what we should call to-day a friendly society; its members afforded each other mutual help. Such Gilds became common in Cambridge as in every town during the Middle Ages; they were the great aids to municipal life, and we shall find that some of them grew rich and powerful enough to found a College on their own account.

Our business is, however, with the University. One cannot fix a deliberate date of foundation. Universities, like every other great design, have small beginnings, and the origin of schools at Cambridge was probably insignificant. Cambridge is on the border of the Fenland, and the Fenland contained the richest abbeys in England. Besides the great house of Ely, where the bishop was by virtue of his office abbot, there were, within easy reach of Cambridge, the four Benedictine abbeys of Peterborough, Ramsey, Thorney and Crowland, all of them in the very first rank of English houses. Life in the Fens was hard and dismal, and even Peterborough, the Medehampstead or Goldenburgh of Saxon times, must have been largely under water for a great part of the year. The towns on the borders, Cambridge or Stamford, formed an excellent asylum for those brethren who were too weak to endure the unhealthy mists of the Nene and Welland Wash. During the middle ages, Cambridge bristled with small religious houses, cells depending on the greater abbeys; and in these the young monks of Crowland and the other houses received their education. This was the beginning of the University. The academic life was the life of the cloister. The teaching consisted of the ordinary medieval sciences, Aristotle and the scholastic logic. In after years, Erasmus deprecated the attachment of Cambridge pedants to Aristotle and their unreadiness to accept the new learning. Cambridge never was quite so famous a nursery of schoolmen as Oxford; her history is somewhat more peaceful. Nor, when the medieval theology fell into discredit, did she produce a teacher with the European fame of Wyclif. Her history, however, has a chronology almost parallel with that of Oxford. Out of the monastic system was evolved the freer life of colleges. Oxford led the way with University and Merton; Cambridge followed with Peterhouse. The college, as distinct from the monastery, was a place of retreat whose aim was learning; the aim of the monastery was self-discipline. It is needless to say that these colleges were established upon a clerical basis: each was a society consisting of a master and a certain number of fellows. Their constitution was that of a public School; the modern undergraduate system was a much later development. The early founders had no idea of a college in the modern sense; a society principally composed of laymen, and a large body of undergraduates who to all intents and purposes are the College. The one link which connects our colleges of to-day with the original foundations is the existence of a college chapel, uniting the various members of the institution for the prime object of the learned society, the glory of God.

Medieval Cambridge lay, as our Cambridge still lies, east of the river, which flowed in a course more or less corresponding to its present direction. It was enclosed by the King's Ditch, a stream at a tangent to the main river. This started from the Mill Pool at the bottom of Silver Street, and was crossed by Trumpington Street at the Trumpington Gate, close to Pembroke. In fact, it followed the present Mill Lane and Downing Street pretty closely, keeping to the left, until it reached Barnwell Gate at the bottom of Petty Cury. From Barnwell Gate it followed the present Hobson Street, ran across Sidney Gardens and down Park Street, skirted Midsummer Common and rejoined the Cam about a hundred and fifty yards below Magdalene Bridge. Within this elliptic space the old town was contained. If you stood at the Round Church, you would see the two familiar main thoroughfares separate as they do to-day. That to the left, Bridge Street and Sidney Street, was called Conduit Street: it led to the King's Ditch at Barnwell Gate. That to the right, St John's Street and Trinity Street, led to the principal medieval foundations. On the right hand of it was the Hospital of St John; on the left the Jewry and All Saints' Church, with its tower projecting over the roadway, like St John Maddermarket's at Norwich. Just beyond on the right was King's Hall, with King's Hall Lane leading to the river. The next turning, St Michael's Lane, the present Trinity

Lane, led in the same direction to Garret Hostel Bridge. In St Michael's Lane was Michael House, and St Michael's and King's Hall Lanes were connected by the narrow and dirty street called Foul Lane. These two colleges and the tortuous lanes connecting them occupied the site of Trinity. The main street, after passing St Michael's Church, came to Great St Mary's Church, and proceeded along King's Parade as High Street. On either side of this thoroughfare was an indiscriminate mass of houses—the great court of King's did not exist. Its site was then a labyrinth of narrow alleys and beetling tenements. A winding lane led across the space now occupied by the lawn east of King's Chapel, to the Schools, and skirting them, ran into the street leading from Michael House to the Mill Pool, called Milne Street. Of this street, which passed Clare and crossed King's where Gibbs' building stands, we still preserve the original course in Queen's Lane. It was connected with the parallel High Street by Piron Lane, which occupied the north side of the court at King's, and St Austin's Lane, which was the modern King's Lane. Several lanes led from Milne Street down to the river. Milne Street was terminated by Small Bridges Street, now Silver Street, which crossed the river from Newnham and joined High Street at St Botolph's Church.

On the other side of High Street the confusion was even worse. Many people can remember the days when the broad thoroughfares on either side of Great St Mary's were filled with tumble-down houses. This picturesque and unsanitary state of things was almost the last remnant of medieval Cambridge. In this rabbit-warren lived many of the tradespeople. The names of the lanes between High Street and the Market Place are sufficient testimony. The Sheerer's Row, north of Great St Mary's, was continued by the Shoemaker's Row, which is now Market Street. The Market Place was so largely blocked up by this dense mass of houses that it occupied not more than half of its present site. In its centre was the Conduit; west of the Conduit was the Cross. The Tolbooth and Prison were on the south of the space, where the Guildhall is. In front of the Tolbooth were the shambles, and, east of this savoury neighbourhood Petty Cury, the Little Cookery, led to Barnwell Gate. From the Market Place, Peas Hill led, as now, to Bene't Street, and Bene't Street led back to High Street, just where King's Parade joins Trumpington Street. Free School Lane, at the back of Saint Bene't's Church and Corpus, was called Luthburgh Lane, and the original buildings of Corpus opened into this and not into Trumpington Street, as at present. Just before reaching Pembroke, High Street was brought to a stop by Trumpington Gate, just as Conduit Street was finished by Barnwell Gate. On the other side of the King's Ditch were the Church of St Peter and the foundation of Peterhouse.

Another point which the visitor to medieval Cambridge would notice would be the abundance of religious houses. Great towns, such as London or Bristol, were well off in this way, but Cambridge could not compare in size with these cities. There are few of these houses whose remains we cannot trace in one or other of the colleges. It became, in the fifteenth century, the fashion to appropriate the monasteries to purposes of learning. All the great colleges absorbed some of these institutions. The chief were outside the King's Ditch. If accounts are true, the monastery of the Augustinian Canons at Barnwell must have formed a splendid object in any prospect of Cambridge. To reach it, one would pass through meadows, with the nunnery of St Mary and St Rhadegund away to the left. In the southern part of Barnwell, beyond Barnwell Gate, was the house of Black Friars, on one side of Preachers' Street, the *faubourg* which stretched outside the town boundaries and formed the southern approach to Cambridge. This friary is now Emmanuel College. Outside Trumpington Gate was a house of Gilbertine Canons; and opposite it was the house of Friars of the Sack, which became incorporated with Peterhouse. In Cambridge itself the Friars were well represented. The Grey Friars occupied the site of Sidney Sussex College; the White Friars, that picturesque order which reckoned Elijah as its patriarch, had a house on part of the site of Queens' College. The Austin Friars lived on a piece of ground very nearly corresponding to the University laboratories, which was entered from Bene't Street, just where that street meets Peas Hill. All these friaries were bounded on one side by water: the Carmelite house met the river; the Franciscan and Augustinian houses abutted on the ditch. Of these monastic buildings in the town we have scarcely any trace; their position is merely distinguishable. The Dominican house was swept away by the founders of Emmanuel, and no one could detect any monastic remains in the prosaic aspect of that eminently Puritan college. At Jesus, however, Alcock successfully preserved the plan of the nunnery; and the college which we see is in substance a monastic building. Barnwell Priory, with the exception of a small chantry-chapel, has disappeared. The Augustinian hospital of St John has been blotted out by St John's College; its beautiful piscina, incorporated in Sir Gilbert Scott's chapel, is its only relic. And, actually, the only building which has been allowed to stand without alteration is the remote and melancholy Lepers' Chapel at Stourbridge, a beautiful Norman building, which was attached to the Hospital of St Mary Magdalene.

Stourbridge is a good mile beyond Jesus College. In the field close by the Leper's Chapel was held the famous Stourbridge Fair, the English counterpart of Beaucaire and Nijni-Novgorod. There is no doubt that the medieval Cambridge owed its fame in a very large measure to this annual mart. It was the most important of a series of fairs in the Eastern Counties—Tombland Fair at Norwich and the marts of Lynn and Wisbech have still a certain celebrity—and its interest is largely enhanced by the fact that, after the dissolution of the leper's hospital, its original proprietor under a charter of King John, the University had an official connection with it. It lasted for a month, from August 24th to September 28th, and during that period received visits from all the principal merchants in England. It was opened by the Vice-Chancellor in person and was patronised, perhaps rather noisily, by the University generally. Its commercial importance is to be gathered from a passage in Defoe's *Tour of Great Britain*, quoted by Mr Atkinson in his interesting account of the fair. Hops and wool were the two great staples of trade, and Stourbridge Fair determined the price of hops in England. It was thus not a mere place of pleasure, but resembled the great nomadic markets of the east. Anybody who has been to Lynn Mart or to Stourbridge Fair itself in its sorry old age knows that to-day the great business of the fairs consists in steam roundabouts and side-shows. The roundabout is a late development, but the side-show has an honourable antiquity. Stourbridge Fair boasted, within the last century, a theatre where legitimate Shaksperian drama was admirably performed by a Norwich company. The performances were largely attended by the University, and enterprising ladies like Mrs Frere of Downing were to be seen there with fashionable parties. The story is often told of "rare Richard Farmer," Master of Emmanuel, how he and a few friends, ardent lovers of Shakspere, attended the Stourbridge Theatre night after night, occupying a bench especially reserved for them.

At Stourbridge Fair University and Town took joint management of the proceedings. They did not, however, love one another very cordially, and the Town resented the rights which the University enforced with some arrogance. "Town and Gown rows" were, in the ordinary course of things, not very common. When they broke out, they were serious; but usually the University was much to blame. For example, in James I.'s time, George Ruggle, fellow of Clare, wrote a play in derision of the town's folk, to which the college, with the worst taste, invited the Mayor and Corporation. But that the town, at any rate in medieval times, watched the growth of the University with favour, is sufficiently proved by the refoundation of Corpus Christi College, the work of townspeople. The University repaid the debt in subsequent years by foundations like Perse's Grammar School and Addenbrooke's Hospital. We must remember that, ecclesiastically, the connection of town and university was for some centuries very close. The church of St Mary by the Market was not merely the chapel of King's Hall; it was also a parish church, and a large and important gild of merchants had their chapel within its walls. At first, the colleges were entirely opposed to the monastic spirit. They did not worship in their own chapels, but joined in the devotions of the ordinary congregations, going to church just as the grammar school of any town in England attends the parish church, as a matter of course. The extreme youth of the scholars completes the comparison. But, as the colleges grew in riches and numbers, they reverted to the monastic ideal, and each built its own chapel. The Town and University drew apart from each other, and the University became the more important body. Moreover, while the learning of the University grew, the trade of the town diminished. The gradual diversion of trade from the Eastern Counties, the decay of ports like Lynn, with whose commerce Cambridge was inseparably linked, all the changes in the physical geography of the Fens, reduced the importance of the town. It would be unfair to assert that Cambridge, as a whole, exists for the sake of the University; but there is no doubt that the nucleus of the town, its whole western quarter, is devoted to that purpose, and that, without the University, it would be of little more importance than Huntingdon or St Ives—of less importance, probably, than Ely or Wisbech, which are still at the head of an excellent water-way.

Cambridge, no less than Oxford, took her part in the religious commotions of the sixteenth century. She was deeply concerned in the revival of learning. She shares with Oxford the honour of enrolling Waynflete and Foxe among the members of the University. Bishop Fisher belongs entirely to her, and, in consequence, Cambridge was the University which the Lady Margaret favoured more conspicuously. Erasmus taught in her schools. Even before the Dissolution, she showed, by her appropriation of religious houses to scholastic purposes, the growth of that liberal spirit which is thought to be her intellectual distinction. We shall see how pious Churchmen like Bishop Alcock and a medieval devotee like Lady Margaret did not scruple to sweep away monasteries for the sake of learning. Even monasteries themselves, in these later days, followed up their own initiative and endowed colleges. Several abbeys united to found Buckingham College. Alcock, by virtue of his episcopal office, was abbot of the great monastery of Ely. In the great struggle which followed the revival of learning as its natural outcome, Cambridge contributed her martyrs to both sides. Fisher died in the defence of a rigid principle. On the other hand, Cambridge prepared those three reformers who suffered for their opinions at Oxford. Cranmer was a fellow of Jesus, Ridley was Master of Pembroke, Latimer belonged to the societies of Christ's and Clare. It is not at all surprising that their influence, combined with the constant importation of Genevan teachers, rendered Cambridge very susceptible for a time to reformed doctrine of a foreign type. But the final result of the Reformation in the University is shown by the intellectual freedom of her greatest sons. Bacon and Sir Isaac Newton are the obvious examples of this, but their illustrious personalities should not allow us to forget the brilliant ingenuity of the Cambridge Platonists; while, side by side with the greatest of all we may place the name of John Milton.

Milton, whose life is very largely bound up with Cambridge, brings us to another critical point in University history. It is difficult to estimate the attitude of Cambridge as a whole to the Civil Wars. Oxford remained faithful to the King, but, while Cambridge possessed no college so unanimously loyal as St John's at Oxford, there were one or two colleges, such as Sidney and Emmanuel, whose sympathies were undeniably Puritan. An University cannot help a certain amount of conservatism, and Cambridge sacrificed a great deal in the Stewart cause. A few years ago, at the exhibition of plate in the Fitzwilliam Museum, one realised the substantial cost of that sacrifice. But the Fens and the whole neighbourhood were devoted to the interest of the Parliament, and there were actually few who surrendered themselves as martyrs to the royalist cause. On the religious side of the question, however, Cambridge has a good deal to show. Some of the most eminent Caroline divines are hers. Lancelot Andrewes, John Cosin, Jeremy Taylor, Peter Gunning, to mention no other names, were all Cambridge men. George Herbert and Nicholas Ferrar were men of some academical distinction. But, if it is true that architecture is the best witness to history, no town in England shows more trace of the Puritan spirit than Cambridge. While the Oxford buildings of the seventeenth century are gravely Gothic and semi-ecclesiastical, the only building of this type in Cambridge is the picturesque chapel at Peterhouse. The library of St John's, beautiful though it is, is a hybrid example of the order. Other seventeenth century work, the work of Ralph Symons, for example, the court of Clare, and Wren's masterpieces at Trinity and Emmanuel, are frankly domestic. Men such as I have mentioned above, belong to a *coterie*, but do not represent the general temper of their age.

During the eighteenth century the state of the University was more or less torpid. It was the age of combination rooms and good port, of hard-and-fast social distinctions and formal gatherings. The Universities, during this period, lost their touch with English life, and were not even the forcing-houses of wit. This is especially true of Cambridge. The first half of the century is absorbed in the great quarrel between Bentley and his society. Bentley is unquestionably the most commanding figure of his time at Cambridge; for Newton by this time belonged chiefly to London. But Bentley was hated by the great company of wits, who had, for the most part, little to do with either University. Pope, Swift, Fielding and Richardson, the four writers who had the greatest influence on their century, were connected with neither Oxford nor Cambridge. And, from 1750 to 1790, there is very little to relieve the general dulness which settled over Cambridge. Mr John Willis Clark, in a delightful and only too short chapter, has revived for us the social etiquette and pleasures of the period. But the pleasures themselves are remarkable, for the most part, for their unconscious humour. And even the epigrams, in spite of their uniform cleverness, are a trifle heavy.

The French Revolution woke Cambridge from this long sleep. It was an active stimulant to the imagination. The fall of the Bastille had its effect upon Wordsworth at St John's and Coleridge at Jesus; its immediate result, the general cry for independence, moved Byron at Trinity. The romantic enthusiasm set in, and with it that love for a liberal education apart from mechanical scholarship which is so prominent a factor in both Oxford and Cambridge to-day. In short, the modern life of the University began; Cambridge began once more to play its part in English intellectual life. Wordsworth and Tennyson, of all poets, have done most to stimulate the minds of their countrymen, and both owe no small portion of their personal influence to Cambridge. And, side by side with this intellectual revival, one cannot fail to notice the spiritual revival inaugurated by the Wesleys at Oxford, and naturalised by Charles Simeon at Cambridge. This simply means the awakening of the University to the other side of her responsibilities. In the Oxford movement, which was the logical result of this revival, Cambridge had very little share. Her traditions were somewhat different from those of Oxford, and her theological tendencies took what is usually known as a "broader" direction. Her position is indicated by the names of F. D. Maurice and Charles Kingsley. At the same time, her school of theology, under Ellicott, Lightfoot, Hort and Westcott, has preserved its scientific basis and cannot be surpassed in any University. And time would fail to tell of what triumphs she has won in other fields. Darwin in biology, Thomson in electricity, Adams in astronomy, are names which tell their own tale. With these main activities, too, others have grown. The energies of the University have been expanded in every direction. The multiplication of open scholarships and prizes, the University Extension system, the foundation of colleges for women, are only a few of the ways in which her influence has been doubled throughout Great Britain. And in all this surely her founders and benefactors have full recompense for their labours—in the love which the University excites in her sons and in the contribution of each member to the corporate action of the whole body.

CHAPTER II

THE UNIVERSITY CHURCH

The Church of St Mary-by-the-Market, better known as Great St Mary's, is, as it stands at present, a fine example of the latest style of English architecture. Two churches, when it was built, had already occupied the site. The first, entirely parochial, was probably built in Norman times, but was burned down in 1290. By that time, however, the University then emerging from its embryonic state into actual life, had begun to use it for its meetings. The church formed, as it were, the earliest Senate House. After the fire, which, like so many medieval catastrophes, was put down to the Jews, the structure was renewed in the style of the period. We find that Thomas de L'Isle, Bishop of Ely, granted a license for the consecration of the High Altar in 1346; and that, in 1351, the consecration took place under his successor, Simon of Langham. The chancel still retains some features of this remodelled church. In the year after the consecration, the Gild of the Blessed Virgin Mary, parishioners of this church, joined with the Gild of Corpus Christi in the foundation of Corpus College; and, in 1342, Edward III. had granted the advowson of St Mary's to the scholars of King's Hall. In this way it happened that, at the subsequent rebuilding of the church, the town, the University, and the college were equally concerned in it. The present building was begun in 1478, when John Morton was Bishop of Ely, and the main structure, roughly speaking, belongs to the period between that year and 1491. It is supposed that, during this reconstruction, the services were held in the chancel, which, presumably, was merely remodelled in the perpendicular manner. The character of the nave is, for its period, strikingly excellent, and the work is not unlike that at St Nicholas, Lynn, and other fine churches in the eastern counties. The surface-ornament in the spandrils of the chancel-arch and nave arcade is exceptionally good, and the depression of the arches is very slight. Characteristically, the piers have no capitals, but a small shaft with a plain capital carries the innermost moulding. But the best feature of the interior is the high, plain clerestory, from which the church originally received its principal light. This forms, as it were, a wall of glass running along the upper storey of the church. Its lowest part is panelled, forming a kind of mock triforium. On the whole, there are few more stately churches of the date in England.

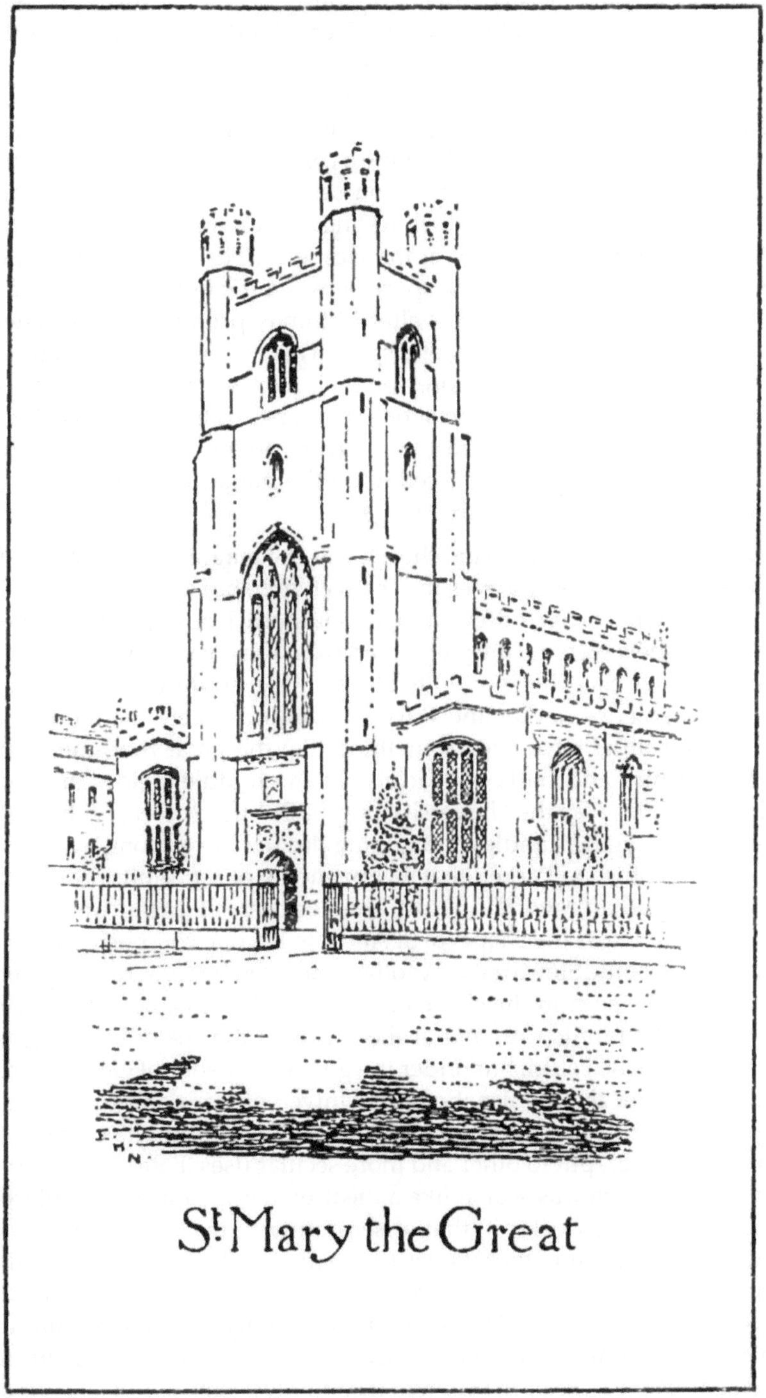

S[t]. Mary the Great

Although this nave was completed in 1491, it was not ready for service till 1519, when the nave was seated and the Great Rood suspended from the chancel-arch. Meanwhile, the tower had been begun in 1491, and progressed very slowly. In 1515 it was at a standstill and had a thatched roof. The west window, however, which, considering that it belongs to Henry VIII.'s reign, is surprisingly good Gothic, was glazed by 1536. After this time a certain amount of work went on, and the tower was carried up to the string-course. In 1576, Sir Walter Mildmay gave twenty tons of freestone towards the building, which was employed in erecting a somewhat heavy Italianised porch at the west end. This, with its great pediment and the clock above it, filled up the space between the buttresses and reached up to the sill of the west window. Sir Walter Mildmay promised other materials for the completion of the tower by a stone spire. This never took place, and, in 1593, the parish decided to add a final storey on their own account, which was completed in 1596. This storey, with its octagonal corner-turrets and debased windows, is nevertheless in no violent contrast to the work below. In 1608, the turrets were completed and stone balls were placed upon the pinnacles by Robert Grumbold, to whom we owe the balls on Clare Bridge.

The last internal addition to the church was the magnificent rood-loft, finished in 1523. It extended not only across the chancel-arch, but across the northern arch, leading to the Chapel of St Andrew, and the southern, leading to the Chapel of Our Lady. These chapels were further separated from the chancel by parclose-screens. The contract states that the rood-lofts at Thriplow, south of Cambridge, and at Gazeley, between Newmarket and Bury St Edmunds, were the models used for this structure. It must have been something like the great rood-lofts which still exist in Devonshire and parts of Norfolk. In the middle, below the rood-beam and facing the choir, was the University pulpit. But this screen, with its elaborate furniture, its "yomages," candles and gilding did not have a long existence. It was destroyed by Archbishop Parker, that sworn enemy of rood-lofts, in 1562. However, during the Laudian revival, in 1640, another chancel-screen was erected, part of which remains across the chapel of St Andrew. Its fine composition and carving are characteristic of the Stewart era. Another and even better screen of a somewhat earlier date is to be seen in the church of Tilney All Saints, near Lynn. However, this screen perished in its turn, not at the hands of the zealot Dowsing, who destroyed as much as he could, but under the gentle influence of Georgian restorers. It appears that, after the Reformation, the University sermon became more of an institution than it had been, and was no longer preached to the chancel. Great St Mary's was, however, put to other and more secular uses. Laud was informed that the body of the church was seated like a theatre; that the pulpit was placed in the middle and called the Cock-pit; that at sermon-time the chancel was filled with boys and townsmen "and other whiles (thereafter as the Preacher is) with *Townswomen* also, all in a rude heap between the Doctors and the Altar"; that the "Service there (which is done by Trin. Coll.) is commonly posted over and cut short at the pleasure of him that is sent thither to read it." Divers other informations were laid against the state of the church. It certainly seems curious to our own day that the Commencements should have been held in church, and that the feeble buffoonery of the "Prevaricator" should have been, under these circumstances, their leading feature. The feeling against these extraordinary ceremonies led to the building of the Senate House, which was large enough for disputations as well as meetings of the senate. But Sir James Burrough, to whom the Senate House is partly due, did his best to spoil the University Church. The screen of 1640, which, with its spirelets and canopies, must have been very like the Laudian screens remaining in one or two northern churches,[1] was taken down; and the church was devoted entirely to the cult of the sermon. Mr William Worts had previously left a legacy to the University, which was employed in erecting the present galleries (1735). The Cock-pit was remodelled, and the centre of the church was filled with an immense octagonal pulpit on the "three-decker" principle, the crowning glory and apex of which was approached, like a church-tower, by an internal staircase. About 1740, Burrough filled the chancel-arch and chancel with a permanent gallery, which commanded a thorough view of this object. The gallery, known as the "Throne" was an extraordinary and unique erection. The royal family of Versailles never worshipped more comfortably than did the Vice-Chancellor and heads of houses, in their beautiful arm-chairs, and the doctors, sitting on the tiers of seats behind them. In this worship of the pulpit, the altar was quite disregarded, and Cole the antiquary remarked sorrowfully on this discreditable fact. Undergraduates, whose power of expression was not equal to their sense of humour, irreverently called the Throne Golgotha, because the heads of houses sat there. The church thus became an oblong box, with the organ at one end, the Throne at the other, and the pulpit between them. The portentous array of bevelled and panelled oak plunged the church in darkness, and so, in 1766, the aisle windows were altered and the present meagre insertions made.

This domestic comfort pervaded the church until 1863. The Camden Society destroyed the picturesque top of the tower in 1842, but did not touch the interior of the church. In 1851 Sir Gilbert Scott took away Mildmay's porch, and substituted for it the present west door. Much about the same time, the ground round St Mary's was cleared of houses. Dr Luard, the late registrary, who was then Vicar, agitated for the removal of the "throne" for a long time, and at last the work of reconstruction began. The present nave-seats and chancel-stalls, in a somewhat florid style, were put in, and the only remains of the old preaching-house were the galleries and the organ at the west end. This organ, which dates from 1698, and is in part the work of Father Smith, was rebuilt by Messrs Hill in 1870. In 1888 the south porch was rebuilt on the lines of a porch which had been destroyed in 1783. Under the present vicar, Dr Cunningham, the work of restoration has advanced. The tower has been thoroughly repaired, and a new organ has been built for parochial services on the south side of the choir. Further, the late Mr Sandars, who did so much for the University, filled in the lower part of the aisle windows with the arms of those noblemen and prelates who subscribed to the nave between 1478 and 1519. These windows, which are by Messrs Powell, are full of interesting matter for the student of monastic heraldry. Messrs Powell are similarly engaged in filling the clerestory windows with admirable figure-glass. Altogether, during the last half-century, the church has returned some way towards its original design. There is now a side altar in St Andrew's Chapel, which is used as the chapel of the

[1] *E.g.* Brancepeth and Sedgefield, Co. Durham.

Clergy Training-School; the Lady Chapel is occupied by the vestry. And, finally, one must not forget the "Cambridge chimes" in the tower, which were composed in 1790 by Dr Jowett of garden fame, and are the model of all such chimes throughout England.

CHAPTER III

PETERHOUSE

From the churchyard of Little St Mary's Church a good idea of the medieval buildings of Peterhouse may be obtained. Unfortunately, James Essex was allowed to do as he liked with the old court somewhere about 1770, and faced it in the hideous, commonplace style of the time. It is astonishing that he allowed the back of the older building, so out of harmony with the cherished classical unities of his day, to remain in so conspicuous a position. But the obvious history of the buildings begins with Dr Andrew Perne's library, whose later extension with its gabled end and oriel is such a picturesque object in the perspective of Trumpington Street, and contrasts so oddly with the Corinthian portico of the Fitzwilliam Museum, just beyond. Perne's work is in that familiar, country-house style which, rather later, we associate in Cambridge with the name of Ralph Symons. The building of 1590 forms the eastern extension of the Hall and Combination Room. It was prolonged in 1632 to stand flush with the present street-pavement. Bishop Matthew Wren made a more notable and more characteristic addition. He built the chapel, which was consecrated in 1632, on a site in the eastern half of the court, just midway between the two wings. At the same time he united his building to the wings by an open cloister supporting a covered gallery. The chapel and cloisters, which divide the court into two unequal halves, have a good deal of picturesqueness, but they are built in a very stilted Italian manner, full of shallow late Gothic detail. The chapel has a considerable reputation founded on its stained glass windows, which are by Professor Aimmüller of Munich. They are astonishing specimens of their art, and reflect the taste of the middle of the century very well. An excellent Flemish east window, contemporary with the building, is usually considered to harmonise very ill with these productions, whose qualities, nevertheless, it considerably enhances.

Under the Georgian *régime* Peterhouse suffered a great deal. Sir James Burrough of Caius, then neither Master nor a Knight, had a grand plan for taking down Perne's library and Wren's cloisters and putting up buildings of his own. Happily, the funds for this undertaking allowed him to finish only the imposing northern wing, next to Little St Mary's Church. Like most of his work, this wing, completed in 1742, is in very good taste, and the influence of Gibbs' building at King's is to be traced throughout. Nearly half a century later came Essex with a neat taste acquired, perhaps, in the neighbourhood of St Marylebone, and made a beautiful structure exceptionally ugly. Last of all, Mr Francis Gisborne's trustees, after his death in 1821, built a new western court in the then fashionable sort of

Gothic with a part of £20,000 bequeathed to the College in his will. This court calls for little remark.

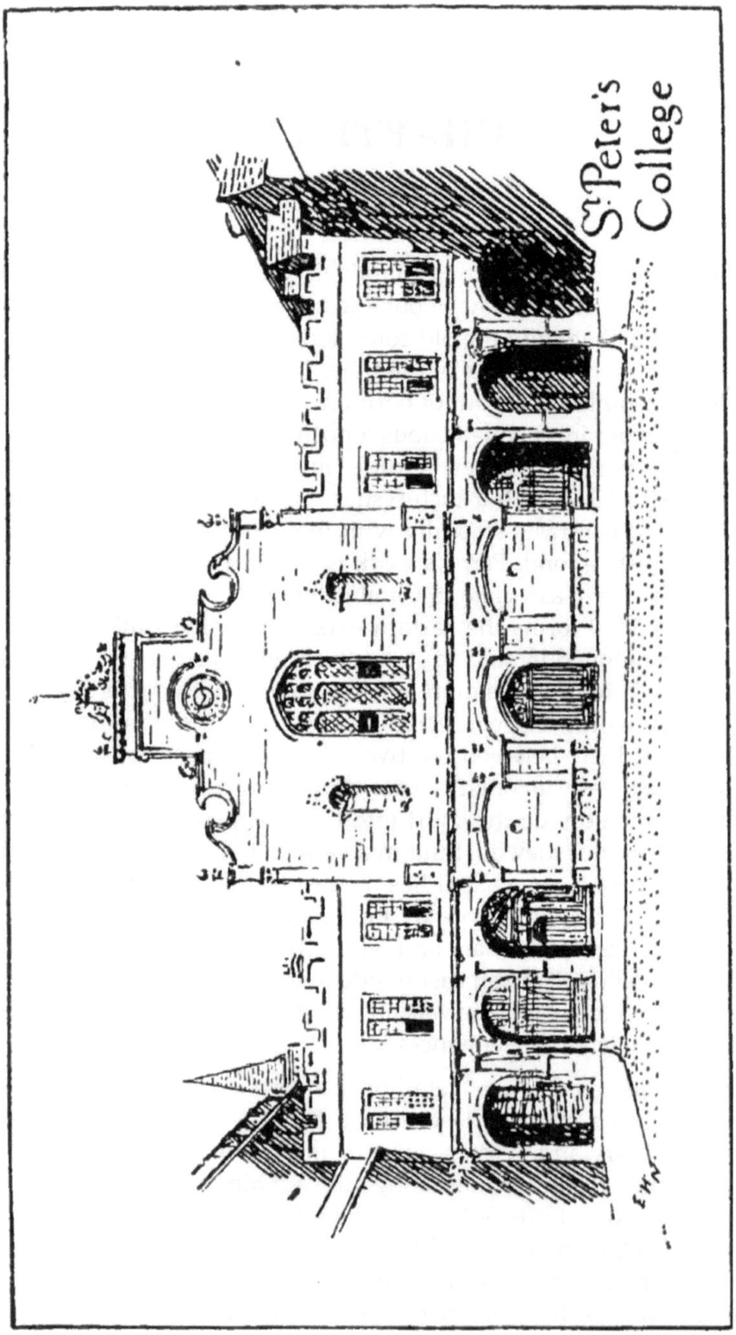

St. Peter's College

Too late to stay the hand of the spoiler, the Gothic revival has nevertheless done much for Peterhouse. Mr Gilbert G. Scott in 1870 rebuilt the Hall and Combination Room and incorporated in them the remains of the medieval Master's Lodge, which had been long ago superseded by the comfortable brick house just across Trumpington Street. Good, unassuming and appropriate work in themselves, these buildings are further decorated with some very successful stained glass by the late Sir Edward Burne-Jones and Mr William Morris. The bright oriel of the Hall is especially beautiful, and the small figures of poets and of the good women of Chaucer's dream in the windows of the comfortable parlour, share, with the chapel glass, the impartial admiration of the visitor. It is satisfactory to think that this historical college has received some compensation for all the damage inflicted on it.

In 1281 Hugh de Balsham, Bishop of Ely, founded St Peter's College. The reign of Edward I. is the date from which our universities derive their organisation, and in many other ways it marks an epoch in English history. Walter de Merton, Bishop of Rochester, had, seventeen years before, founded Merton College at Oxford.[2] It was therefore emulation which, to a certain extent, inspired Hugh de Balsham in his new departure. He was a native of Cambridgeshire: his native place is about ten miles distant from Cambridge, on the confines of Essex; and he had probably received his education in one of the numerous religious houses which filled the Cambridge of that period. As Bishop of Ely, and therefore as titular abbot of the monastery, he had much to do with the monastic institutions of the town, and it was only natural that, with Walter de Merton's example before his eyes, he should wish to make his name famous in the same way. He lived just long enough to see the college established and in a fair way to success, with a master and fourteen scholars in residence. His successors at Ely continued his favours to the college, and during the next century we find the names of Bishops Simon Montague, Thomas de L'Isle, Simon Langham and John de Fordham among the benefactors. It is interesting to note how purely local University education must have been at first. Although the first two masters of Peterhouse appear to have been natives of distant parts of England, the names of most of the masters during the fourteenth century recall the neighbouring fenland. Roger of Mildenhall, Ralph of Holbeach, William of Whittlesea, Richard of Wisbech, John of Bottisham, all are natives of Cambridgeshire or the counties immediately adjoining. Thomas of Barnard's Castle, who became master in 1400, takes us further north, and he is the last of the list who derives his surname from his native place.

The early history of Peterhouse is concerned chiefly with its buildings. Under the rule of John Holbrook (1418-1431) and during the long mastership of Dr Thomas Lane (1431-73) the college assumed a definite shape. The old buildings north of it belong to Holbrook's mastership. It took in the house of the Friars of the Sack, which existed on part of its site, and thus set a precedent which was followed

[2] Merton College was founded in 1264, but its corporate existence does not actually begin till 1274. Similarly, Peterhouse, founded in 1281, did not possess buildings or enjoy a common life till 1284, the year of Hugh de Balsham's death.

almost universally—the substitution of learned foundations for monasteries and convents. The Peterhouse of that day, substantially the building of our own time, was scarcely in Cambridge. St Peter's Church lay north of it, and was itself just outside the Trumpington or South Gate of the town. It had given its name to the college, and was used as its chapel from the earliest period. About the beginning of Edward III.'s reign, the church was pulled down, and the present beautiful church of St Mary's the Less was built on its site, the college still continuing to use it as their place of worship. We may assume that the scholars were required to assist at mass every morning and at the parochial mass on Sundays, and that they formed, as it were, the choir, using the chancel stalls. They entered the church by the passage and staircase which still exist south of the chancel.

No famous names occur in connection with the college before the Reformation. The early sixteenth century produced a good number of benefactors, and Hugh de Balsham's original provisions were considerably amplified. In 1553 Andrew Perne became master. His fame is largely local, but he is a very significant figure in an age chiefly remarkable for the strength of its religious convictions. His mastership begins at the end of Edward VI.'s reign, and lasted for thirty-six years. He combined with it the Deanery of Ely, and showed great sagacity in the tenure of both offices. During Mary's reign, he was Chancellor of the University, and under his auspices the burning of Bucer's and Fagius' remains took place. However, although this somewhat unnecessary act of vengeance might have stamped his opinions, he seems to have veered at the accession of Elizabeth with great suppleness, and to have trimmed his sails to the royal wind up to the day of his death. The wits of the University made his accommodating policy their butt, and, with the heavy wit of the day, coined the verb *pernare*, which signified "to turn one's coat." Perne, although he possibly merits some contempt, made nevertheless a very good use of his unscrupulous comfort. I have already mentioned his additions to the college. He also originated that water-supply which is now so ornamental a feature in certain parts of the town. The broad gutters along which streams run down Trumpington Street for most of the year were not constructed till after his death, but it was he who first suggested that healthy water might be brought from the neighbouring Gogmagog Hills.

To the society of Peterhouse, for some years of Perne's time, belonged the celebrated John Whitgift. Whitgift was an example of a system which has now ceased to a great extent in Cambridge. He was an undergraduate of Queens' to begin with; he then obtained a fellowship at Peterhouse, and was in succession Master of Pembroke and Trinity before his elevation to a bishoprick. His connection with Peterhouse is very passing, but, while a member of the college, he held the Lady Margaret Professorship of Divinity. In 1567, when he became Master of Pembroke, he vacated it for the Regius Professorship, which he held until his translation to the See of Worcester. At the same time Peterhouse held also another professor, Dr Thomas Lorkin, who occupied the Regius Chair of Physic. Professorships were then commonly held with other offices, and John Richardson, fellow of Emmanuel, who was Master of Peterhouse from 1609 to 1615 was also Regius Professor of Divinity.

Richardson became Master of Trinity in 1615. In the time of his successor, Thomas Turner, one of Peterhouse's most celebrated sons was in residence, the poet Richard Crashaw. The beginning of the sixteenth century found many poets at Cambridge, of whom Crashaw is certainly not the least remarkable. Like George Herbert, who was some twenty years his senior, he was brought up in the traditions of the Church of England, but scarcely had time to prove his principles before the outbreak of the Civil War. He was by temperament a mystic, and his early love-poems show a certain religious tendency. It is probable that his study of St Theresa and the bigotry of the Puritan party drove him, between them, into the Church of Rome. He eventually took orders and died as a Canon of Loreto. His mystical poems have become very fashionable of late years, and he certainly deserves a very high place among our lyric poets. He was also a musician. Although we know little of his life at Cambridge, it is certain that he must have been a prominent figure in the intellectual life of a period when University life was entirely intellectual.

In 1632 the chapel was finished and was consecrated in the next year by Bishop Francis White of Ely. Next year the master, Dr Matthew Wren, was succeeded by Dr John Cosin. The new master was one of the most acute theologians of the century, and was deeply impressed, like most contemporary churchmen, with the possibilities of the Church of England. He was one of the first to vindicate its position and maintain its orders as valid. His proceedings at Peterhouse were hardly popular. Cambridge has never been guilty of over-rating external forms of worship, and, in the case of Cosin, she showed her indignation very plainly. The Puritans were furious at his ritual; they complained of his bowings and genuflexions, and of the crucifix he set up over the altar of his chapel. In 1643 the iconoclast Dowsing paid a visit to Cambridge, and used the most drastic remedies at Peterhouse. Fortunately, the beautiful east window, which would have provoked his zealous wrath, was hidden by the Society and escaped damage. Cosin was ejected by Parliament in 1644, and for sixteen years the college was ruled by Lazarus Seaman. Cosin returned at the Restoration, and the "idols" were restored to their proper place. But in the same year Cosin was rewarded for his long exile with the See of Durham. In the magnificent chapel which he built at Auckland Castle, we may trace in some measure his affection to Peterhouse; for its beautiful late Gothic was doubtless suggested by Dr Wren's chapel.

Cosin has had no very conspicuous successors. He was the last Master of Peterhouse but one who became a bishop. His immediate predecessors, Leonard Maw and Matthew Wren, were both translated to bishopricks: Maw to Bath and Wells, and Wren, whose name is most famous, to Ely. During the time of Dr Law,* Bishop of Carlisle, who was master from 1754 to 1788, and filled for a short time the chair of Moral Philosophy, the poet Gray was obliged to change his residence to Pembroke. Gray is one of those persons, uncommon in the last century, who saw beauty in nature, and he became a kind of artistic apostle at Cambridge. This position, which usually connotes a superiority amounting to superciliousness, did not render him popular at Peterhouse. He had a horror of fire, and kept a fire-escape attached to his window. One night, some of the more normal members of the college raised an alarm of fire, and Gray descended his fire-escape into a bucket of water which had been prepared for him. Having all that lack of humour which is distinctive of æsthetic reformers, he migrated to Pembroke, where he seems to have been better appreciated than in his own college. He lived in Pembroke for the last twenty-five years of his life, and, for the last three (1768-71), was Regius Professor of Modern History.

Dr Law died in 1788, and was succeeded by Dr Francis Barnes,* who continued in his seat for fifty years, holding, like his predecessor, the Professorship of Moral Philosophy from 1813 to his death in 1838. Then Dr Hodgson was master for nine years, and his successor, Dr Cookson, was succeeded in 1876 by the present Master. Among the notable men of the present day Peterhouse claims the Archbishop of York and Lord Kelvin.* Through Lord Kelvin's generosity, it was the first college in Cambridge to use electric light. None of the rest have adopted this modern improvement till quite recently, and even now it is by no means general. Peterhouse, however, has kept up its traditions and occupies a leading place in the history of scientific progress: for, beside Lord Kelvin, its books contain the names of the mathematician Dr Routh* and the well-known Professor Dewar (* Orchardson).

CHAPTER IV

CLARE COLLEGE

Loggan, in his invaluable *Cantabrigia Illustrata,* gives us two views of the court of Clare, the first a bird's-eye view of the whole building, the second an elevation of the north side, as it was completed at the end of Queen Anne's reign. The college had to pass through some trouble before its buildings were completed. After its foundation in 1342, a court was built which lasted till 1525. It was then injured by fire. The remains were taken down, and preparations were made for a new building, which was not begun till 1638, an unfortunate period. During the Civil Wars, the work was at a standstill, and the north side, built principally during the mastership of Dr Samuel Blythe (1678-1713), was not actually finished till 1715. Sir George Downing, then a fellow commoner, contributed to its completion. Later, in 1769, the present Chapel was built from the designs of the Master of Caius, Sir James Burrough. Clare thus presents examples of three distinct periods in Renaissance work. The earliest portion is the eastern side of the court with the gateway, the beauty of which cannot be too highly praised. The style is the fantastic Italian Gothic of the period, mixed largely with classical forms; but the work is free from what Mr Ruskin would call insincerity. It is useful to compare it with the chapel at Peterhouse, consecrated five years before this was begun. Its characteristics are those of all the cultured work of the early Stewart period, and have points in common with a building like Ingestre Hall near Stafford, which has unfortunately perished by fire. The south side is of the same date; the admirable proportions of this part of the court may be seen from the grounds of King's. On the western side is a building of the time of Charles II. and James II. Its inner face harmonises fairly well with the rest, but debased forms, such as the meaningless broken arch, appear. The river front is pure Palladian, and the effect of the order of pilasters which runs through the two upper stories is very harsh. The northern face of the court is good, solid, ugly Queen Anne work, which has, of late years, been spoiled rather than improved. On this side is the Hall with great sash-windows, which the famous Clare creeper does not succeed in hiding. The Chapel is a plain building of excellent proportions. Internally, it has most of the virtues and faults of a Georgian college chapel: the domical antechapel is an original feature. On the whole, Clare, which covers less ground than most colleges, is, architecturally, among the best; but it is a pity that all was not carried out in the style of the western side, which is almost unrivalled in any country, considering its date. The celebrated bridge, not unlike the Kitchen Bridge at St John's, belongs to the reign of Charles I. and is therefore contemporary with the older part of the court. It is well set off by its charming surroundings. The architect of this bridge, completed in 1640, was Robert Grumbold, who was master-mason to the college, and worked at Great St Mary's as well as at Clare.

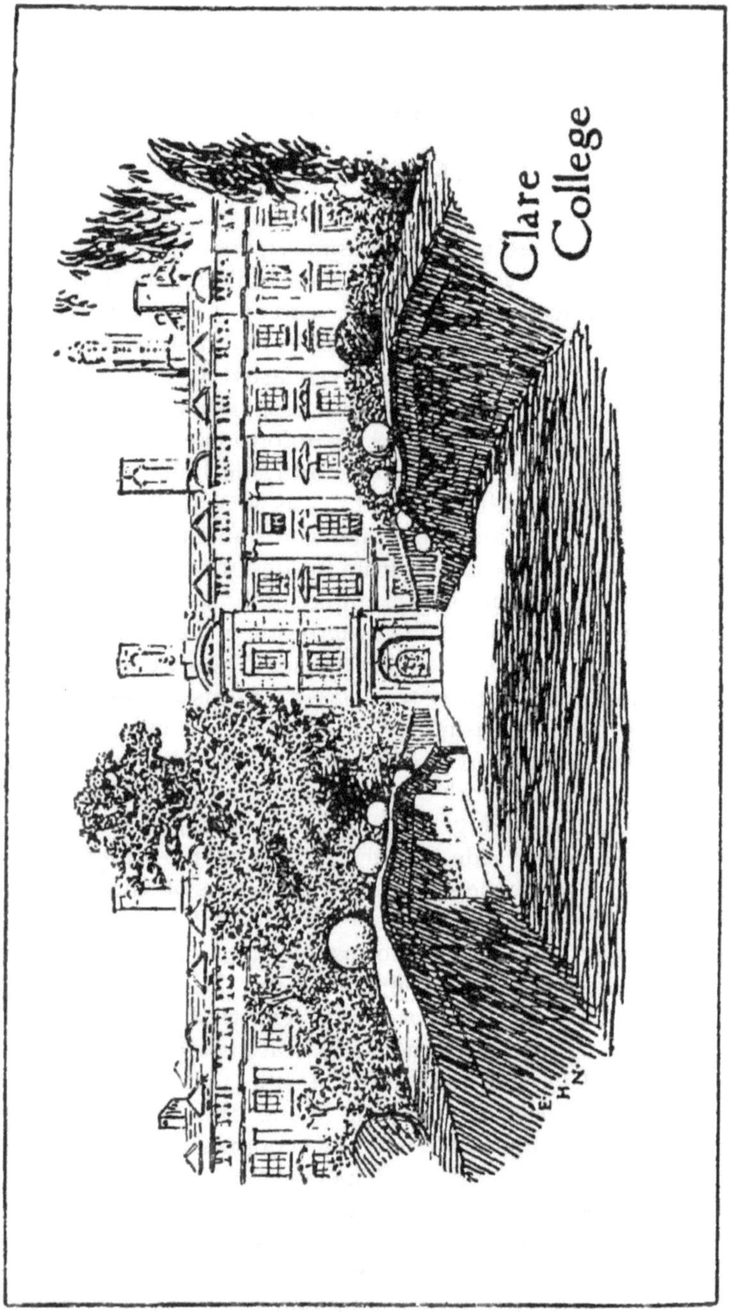

Clare College

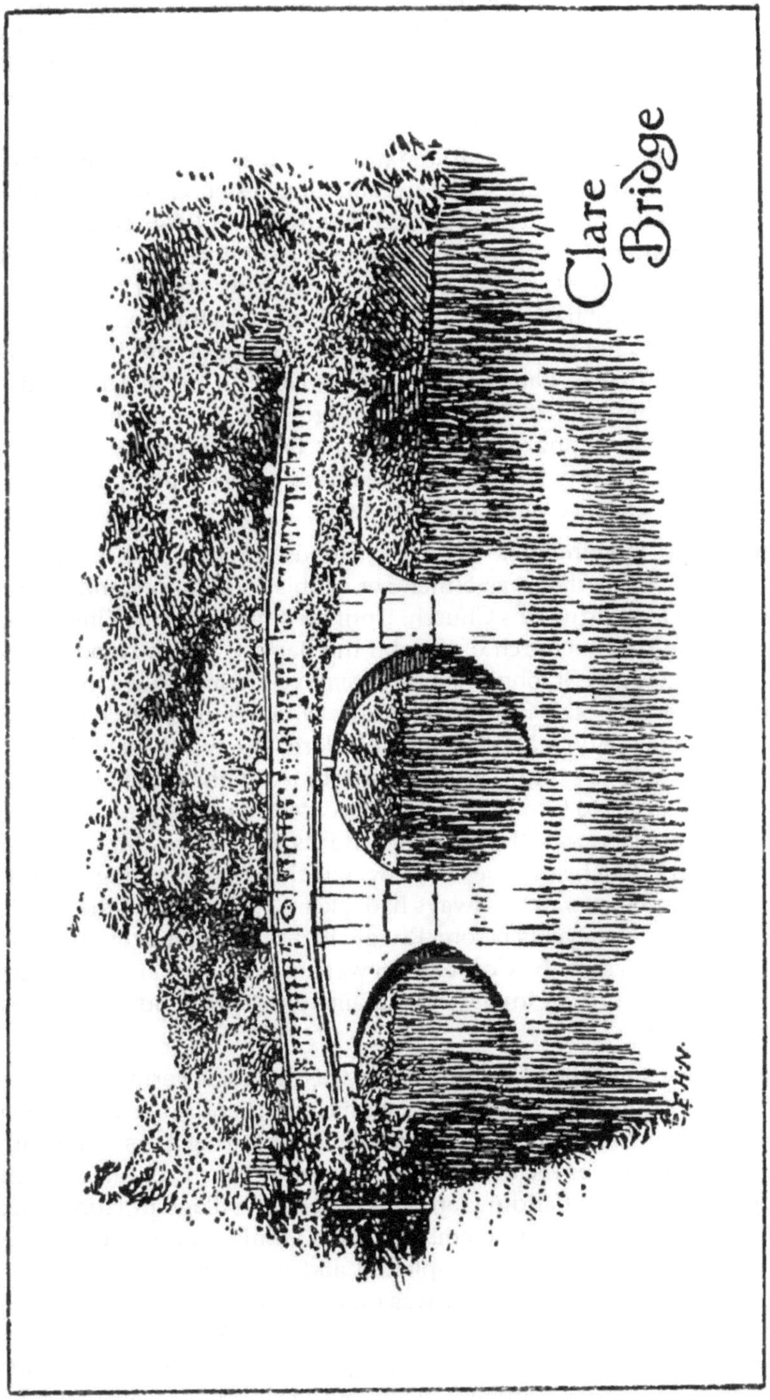

Clare Bridge

The idea of Clare Hall originated with Richard de Badew, who, in 1326, while Chancellor of the University, founded a small college called University Hall. The first master of this new foundation was Walter of Thaxted. But, in the twelfth year of its existence, the college was burned down. Usually the present college dates its foundation from 1338, when the rebuilding began, but the actual date at which Elizabeth de Burgh took over the foundation was 1342. She was daughter and co-heir of Gilbert, Count of Clare, Hertford and Gloucester. Clare lies on the border of Suffolk and Essex, and the college was essentially an Essex colony. Two of the early masters, Walter of Thaxted and William of Radwinter, came from villages in the same part of the county, and their names, occurring not far apart, argue a certain feeling in favour of natives of the district. There was for a long time a tradition that Clare Hall was the Soler Hall of Chaucer's *Reve's Tale*, but it is not necessary to suppose that Chaucer had any particular college in his mind. His use of the epithet "great" may point to Clare and distinguish it from the numerous hostels which were then springing up in Cambridge; but there can be no certainty on the point. Chaucer merely borrowed a tale from Boccaccio and put it into English dress, without any particular accuracy of detail.

Clare has, on the whole, no very momentous annals. Hugh Latimer,* the famous Bishop of Worcester, was a member of this foundation, and, as Fellow of Clare, preached in St Edward's Church. Until the foundation of King's, the chapel of Clare was the parish church of St John the Baptist, which stood on the south side of the college. After St John's had been removed to make way for King's, Clare shared the possession of St Edward's Church with Trinity Hall. Latimer, however, is by no means the typical theologian of Clare. The worthies of the college are chiefly religious, and, a century after, it contributed to the Laudian revival. When James I. paid his visit to Cambridge, he was entertained with a comedy at Clare. The name of the piece was "Ignoramus" and its author was Mr George Ruggle, one of the society. It satirised the civil law, which was then doing its best to oust the canon law, and James, who always had a keen sympathy for the obsolete, was hugely delighted. Some years before, Ruggle had satirised the townsfolk in a play called *Club-Law,* to which the Corporation were invited. The absence of good feeling which marked such an invitation explains the "town and gown rows" common at this period.

A less festive spirit than George Ruggle was Nicholas Ferrar,* who appears at Clare about the same time. Ferrar ranks with Herbert and Crashaw as the third of the mystics and pietists whom Cambridge sent out during the seventeenth century. He became famous as the head of what he called the "Protestant Nunnery." It was established at Little Gidding, an out-of-the-way village in Huntingdonshire, and consisted of Ferrar, some members of his family, and some near relations, who devoted themselves to contemplation and works of piety. The neighbourhood of Little Gidding to Cambridge was probably felt in the University, and there is the strongest probability that men like Cosin and Andrewes came over from Cambridge very often, and went into retreat, as we say, with Ferrar. A man of this type was the great Peter Gunning,* Fellow of Clare and Lady Margaret Professor of Divinity. In 1661 he exchanged his offices for those of Regius Professor and

Master of Corpus, which he soon left for St John's.

While the new court of Clare was building, the Commonwealth came, and with it the mastership of Ralph Cudworth. This profound thinker held the chair of Hebrew with his mastership, and continued to hold it till his death in 1688. He is certainly one of the most extraordinary figures of his age at Cambridge, but his history and that of the band whose leader he was, belong more properly to the annals of Christ's. Almost a contemporary of Cudworth's was Archbishop Tillotson,* who, at this date in his career, was a Puritan, like many of the youth at Cambridge. He later found his true vocation in the Church of England, and his sermons have achieved a greater fame than Cudworth's abstract treatises, although their merits are perhaps less.

Theophilus Dillingham succeeded Cudworth, and was Archdeacon of Bedford as well as master. He continued the buildings, and a successful completion was reached under the subsequent mastership of Samuel Blythe. From this time forward the history of Clare was peaceful and monotonous. It produced a very eccentric son in William Whiston, known as the admirable translator of Josephus. Whiston was an astronomer and a proficient mathematician. He preceded Sir Isaac Newton as Lucasian Professor, resigning his chair in 1711. He was always open to the influence of new and uncommon theories, and died a Baptist with a strong tendency to Fifth-Monarchy principles.

Clare was the college of that famous statesman, Thomas Holles Pelham,* Duke of Newcastle, whose personal peculiarities are ridiculed in Smollett's *Humphrey Clinker*. Pelham was Chancellor of the University from 1748 to 1768, having previously filled the office of High Steward. His Chancellorship is the last important event in the history of the College. It has, since then, under the fortunate and prolonged rule of four masters, extending over a century and a half, maintained its ancient prestige, and now, although one of the smallest of the colleges in point of buildings, the number of its undergraduates is exceptionally large and shows no signs of decreasing. Among its present members it numbers several men of great eminence, of whom, to Cambridge men, the most familiar is the present Woodwardian Professor, Dr McKenny Hughes.

CHAPTER V

PEMBROKE COLLEGE

Modern architects have taken such delight in seeing what can be done with Pembroke that we have scarcely any vestiges of the old building. The long, low street front of the first court, a reminiscence of Oxford, with its double oriel, was refaced in 1726. It was the era of Gibbs and Burrough, and the treatment is therefore thoroughly conservative. But since then, Archbishop Rotherham's fine, monastic plan has been ruthlessly spoiled. The oldest existing part is the Ivy Court, a pretty double range of rooms at the back of the Hall. The north side dates from 1633; the south, or Hitcham Building, from 1659, at which period Rotherham's Library still formed the upper storey of the Hall, and the Chapel stood in the north-west corner of the first court. Bishop Wren's chapel superseded the latter building after the Restoration. It was consecrated in 1667, and is in curious contrast with the same prelate's chapel of 1632 at Peterhouse. His nephew, the great Sir Christopher Wren, was the architect of this building and the adjoining cloister, which is so pleasant a feature of the western side of the court. Wren's genius is clearly visible in the stately unpretentious exterior; but inside, the chapel is cold and ineffective. Stained glass of the type which has been employed at the east end of St Paul's Cathedral, is wanted to complete the design.

Pembroke escaped Essex and Wilkins, but it can hardly be congratulated on what it has acquired instead. The south side of the old court has perished; the quaint two-storied building which contained the Hall and Library, has disappeared, and, instead, we have the modern Hall, a very insignificant Gothic apartment quite out of keeping with the traditions of Pembroke. Mr Waterhouse's street front, south of the chapel, is quite the worst modern building in Cambridge so far as appearance goes; his library and clock-tower are, fortunately, in a not very obtrusive position. Of late years, Mr G. G. Scott has built a very pretty court in a French Renaissance style at the back of the college, where Downing Street meets Tennis Court Lane, but, in building the Laboratory opposite in precisely the same style, he has committed an error which he would have done well to avoid. This court belongs to 1883; the Master's Lodge, between it and the rest of the college, is by Waterhouse, and was finished ten years earlier.

Pembroke College

"O Domus antiqua et religiosa!" said Queen Elizabeth, as she passed by the gates of Pembroke Hall. Very few colleges deserve the epithet better, for Pembroke has been one of the most religious of all Cambridge foundations, and its history is closely connected with the Church. Like Clare, Pembroke owes its origin to a woman. Marie de St Paul, daughter of Guy, Count of St Paul and Châtillon, married Aymer de Valence, Earl of Pembroke. There is a legend that the Earl was killed at a tournament on his wedding day, and Gray embodied the tradition in his noble Installation Ode—

> "Sad Châtillon, on her bridal morn,
> That wept her princely love."

History, however, has made short work with this story. At all events, after her husband's death, the Countess retired from the world, and, among other charitable works, founded Pembroke Hall or, as she called it, the Hall of Valence-Mary. This name did not continue long in use; the college was very soon known, on the analogy of Clare, as Pembroke Hall, and the title of College was given to it in the last century. The foundation dates from 1347, when a Master, fifteen scholars and four Bible-clerks were established on the present site. Robert de Thorpe was first master.

Pembroke is intimately connected with the revival of learning in England. Henry VI. contributed generously to the foundation, and practically set it upon a new footing. Laurence Booth, who became master in 1450 and held the office until his death, was a man of great learning. His ecclesiastical promotion was rapid; he became Bishop of Durham in 1457, and Archbishop of York in 1476. Thomas Rotherham* succeeded him as Archbishop of York and Master of Pembroke. Rotherham, whose actual surname was Scott, was one of the most active promoters of learning in England. He had previously filled the sees of Rochester and Lincoln, and was Archbishop of York for twenty-one years. While Bishop of Lincoln, he had built the east side of the University Library, and he became the second founder of Lincoln College at Oxford. As Lord Chancellor of England, his political career was stormy. Fuller, in speaking of his library at Pembroke, says "Many have mistaken this for the performance of Richard the Third, merely because his Crest the *Boar* is set up therein. Whereas the truth is that *Rotheram* having felt the sharp Tuskes of that *Boar* (when imprisoned by the aforesaid King for resigning the Great Seal of England to Queen Elizabeth, the relict of King Edward the Fourth) advanced his arms thereon that he might ingratiate himself." Rotherham fell on more peaceful days when Henry VII. came to the throne. He resigned the mastership in 1488, and died of the plague at Cawood in 1501.

Curiously enough, the next master but two, Richard Foxe (* copy of Oxford pictures) founded Corpus Christi College at Oxford, just as Rotherham had re-founded Lincoln. He was at that time Master of Pembroke and Bishop of Winchester. Foxe was one of the greatest prelates of that great age. His benefactions to learning were innumerable and priceless; three colleges at Oxford and three at Cambridge count him among their benefactors; his splendid chantry at Winchester, one of the finest pieces of Renaissance sculpture which we possess, is entirely characteristic of this princely ecclesiastic. His enlightened religious views made him the friend and patron of the great scholars who flourished during the reign of Henry VII. He was also remarkable for his political activity; he was the chief agent in the establishment of the Tudor dynasty, and was one of the supporters of the throne against Perkin Warbeck's rebellion. Ford, in his historical drama of *Perkin Warbeck,* drew Foxe's character with admirable force. He died in 1528, old and almost blind, but still retaining all his vigour and adhering to his bishoprick with great tenacity. Foxe may be regarded as one of our earliest and wisest Reformers: he died too early for the final quarrel with Rome, but there can hardly be any doubt that he would have exerted his influence to prevent a formal breach.

A reformer of a different kind was Nicholas Ridley,* master from 1540 to 1553, and Bishop of London during the last three of these thirteen years. It is easy to see the tendencies which the enthusiasm of Rotherham and Foxe for the New Learning had directed, in the fact that Bradford* and Rogers, also martyrs for Protestantism, were members of this college. After Elizabeth's accession, Edmund Grindal,* a Protestant of a somewhat extreme type, became master for three years, during which, like Ridley, he held the see of London. He resigned the mastership in 1562. In 1570 he was translated from London to York, and in 1575 became Archbishop of Canterbury. His successor at Pembroke was the equally famous Matthew Hutton, a learned theologian. His life was closely connected with Cambridge; he took his bachelor's degree in 1551, and ten years later, became Margaret Professor. Becoming head of Pembroke in the following year, he obtained the Regius Professorship of Divinity. He also was married twice to ladies of the neighbourhood. His first wife, Katherine Fulmetby, was niece to Bishop Goodrich of Ely; his second, Beatrice Fincham, also came from Ely. In 1567 he was made Dean of York and left Pembroke. His preferment was almost entirely due to his scholastic disputations before Elizabeth on her visit to Cambridge. While at York, he married a third time, with the true zeal of a post-Reformation prelate for the married state. He was made Bishop of Durham in 1589 and was translated to York in 1594. His effigy, brilliantly painted and attired in the costume of an Elizabethan prelate, stands upright against the south wall of the choir at York Minster.

Whitgift's mastership, lasting for a few months in 1567, gives another Archbishop to Pembroke. But he soon left the college for Trinity. Twenty-two years later, Lancelot Andrewes* became master. As Bishop successively of Chichester, Ely and Winchester, his name is familiar to students of the Laudian movement. He was one of those great men who, by their spirituality rather than their energy, vindicated the Church of England from Papal claims on one side and from Genevan doctrine on the other. He is buried, as is well known, in the Collegiate Church of St Saviour at Southwark. His influence is noticeable in the characters of his immediate successors. Samuel Harsnet, master from 1605 to 1616, was also Bishop of Chichester from 1609 to 1619 and of Norwich from 1619 to 1629; and distinguished himself in all these offices by his peaceful and devout spirit. Nicholas Felton,* Bishop of Bristol, was master from 1616 to 1618, and Bishop of Ely from 1619 to 1628. His next successor but one, Benjamin Laney,* was a stout Royalist, and was conspicuous for his fidelity to the exiled King during the Commonwealth. At the Restoration, he received much recompense. He was made Bishop of Peterborough in 1660, Bishop of Lincoln in 1663, and Bishop of Ely in 1667. This unique example of promotion in the Eastern sees closes the list of Pembroke bishops for some time. Since then, the most famous prelate connected with the college has been Edward Maltby,* Bishop of Chichester in 1831 and of Durham from 1836 to 1856. He was the first of the Bishops of Durham under the regulations by which at the death of Bishop Van Mildert, the Prince-Bishoprick was finally disestablished.

While these "men of much motion and promotion" were occupying the mastership of the college, the foundation was not without its famous sons. They are not, however, very many, and the chief lustre of the college seems to have found its centre in the master. Richard Crashaw was in residence here for some time, doubtless attracted by the saintly fame of the masters of the Stewart epoch. But undoubtedly the greatest son of the college is Edmund Spenser,* who entered the house probably during Hutton's mastership. Of this splendid name Pembroke may well be proud, although it has no very intimate relation with the life of the University. Bishop Matthew Wren,* Master of Peterhouse, was a fellow here. His benefactions are remarkable; they include the fine chapel. He also bequeathed his silver mitre to the College; and this, although somewhat ugly in itself, is one of the most valuable pieces of plate in Cambridge.

Passing over the age of Anne and George I. we come to the long mastership of Dr Roger Long (* Benj. Wilson) who ruled the college from 1733 to 1770. Long became Lowndean Professor of Astronomy in 1750. His astronomical studies were commemorated at Pembroke by a hollow sphere of metal, which had a diameter of eighteen feet and was a complete guide to the solar system. It was contained in a building which terminated the north side of the second court, but it was destroyed in 1871. Dr Long was also much interested in the liberal arts; he was a musician and mechanic; he was also a wit of a not very refined order. His "Musick Speech" delivered in Great St Mary's at the Commencement of 1714, is quoted in Mr J. W. Clark's book on Cambridge. He was then fellow of his college. As master, he was a friend of Thomas Gray. When that sensitive poet left Peterhouse, he met with a royal reception at Pembroke, which proves that the college was progressive in the direction of culture. Gray joined the society, and resided in the second court for fifteen years. His rooms were famous for their comfort in a day when no one thought of furnishing a room with more than a table and a few chairs, and the blue pots in his window were the wonder of Cambridge. He was devoted to his adopted college, and the influence of its structure may be traced in several passages of his poems. From 1768 to 1771, he held the chair of Modern History. There are one or two portraits of him in the college. That by Benjamin Wilson, now in the Combination Room, was painted after his death. Another poet, his close friend and personal admirer, William Mason (* Reynolds) belonged to the society for many years, and died in 1797.

If among poets Pembroke claims Spenser, she can also claim William Pitt among statesmen. There are two portraits of the illustrious Prime Minister, one, by Harlow, in the Hall; the other, by Gainsborough, in the Combination Room. Pitt is, however, the property not so much of a single college as of the University, whose politics have been largely directed by his memory. His name is preserved in the Pitt Club, which was established soon after his death and took his coat of arms. It is to-day the best social club in the University, and has rooms in Jesus Lane. In later years, Pembroke elected John Couch Adams (* Herkomer), the discoverer of Neptune, to a fellowship, thus adding to a list which, if not long, is at least highly distinguished. Under the mastership of Dr Searle (* Ouless), who was elected in 1880, it has become an exceedingly popular college, and its numbers are very largely augmented. Dr Edward Bickersteth, the late Bishop of the Church of England in Japan, was among the most celebrated of its recent members, and held an Honorary Fellowship. The present Bishop of Wakefield is the latest addition to its roll of prelates.

CHAPTER VI

GONVILLE AND CAIUS COLLEGE

The arrangement of buildings at Caius is rather curious, and no Cambridge college has been so transformed since its foundation. The chapel is between the two lesser courts; the hall is at the back of everything, and its position is far from obvious. Caius may be said to consist of two halves: the first half, to the east, borders Trinity Street, and is the New Court; the second and westerly half is an oblong bounded on three sides by narrow lanes and on the other by the rest of the college. This second half is again split into two halves, the northern of which, nearest Trinity Lane, is Gonville Court, and represents the ancient college removed here in 1353 from the other end of King's Parade. Beneath its somewhat modern front an immense quantity of the original work still exists, and fourteenth-century windows have been discovered. The old hall and chapel have disappeared, although part of the present chapel may belong to the original buildings. Caius, however, in refounding the college, altered everything. He built an additional court, south of the ancient college. This, too, has been refaced, and is, for the most part, a comfortable quadrangle of Queen Anne date. But the gates which Caius, giving play to a strange fancy, built for his college, are still entire. His Gate of Humility, a mere postern in the outer buildings, exists no longer; but Mr Waterhouse preserved the idea in his new building, and recently his gate has, in accordance with the founder's design, been made once again the principal entrance. The Gate of Virtue, leading from the new court into Caius Court, is a tall Italian building, in which Gothic and Renaissance forms are most curiously blended. The Italian appearance of the design is due, no doubt, to the corner turret, which introduces a very picturesque element into a simple plan.

While the Gate of Virtue subordinates its ornament to general effect, the last gate, the Gate of Honour, leading appropriately to the Senate House and schools, attracts by beauty of detail. It was finished in 1574, the year after Caius' death, and its design, the heavy architrave with an Ionic order, and the hexagonal, domed structure at the top, is purely classical. It is the most charming building of its date in England, and is a good instance of that love of mere fancy which marks the builders of the late Italian Renaissance. Caius' architect was a certain Theodore Have of Cleves in the Rhenish provinces, who also remodelled the chapel between this and Gonville's court, and probably designed the sarcophagus in which Caius is buried. The bell-tower of the chapel, which agrees very well with the two gateways, is comparatively new. It is worth while to enter the chapel, which, although, after numerous alterations, it is of no particular date or style, has a very pleasant interior, and, in addition to Caius' monument, contains that of Dr Perse, the founder of the Perse Free School in Cambridge. This excellent gentleman, who died in 1617, built most of the original entrance court of the college, in which Caius' Gate of Humility was incorporated. In Loggan's beautiful view of Caius, these buildings seem to have been of the same style as those in the second court of St John's College, the style of which Ralph Symons built so many delightful examples in Cambridge. They belong to 1617. The portion of this court south of the Gate of Humility was built in 1619, in accordance with the will of a late master, Dr Legge.

In 1719, the older courts were faced and the chapel was newly decorated. This work was continued at intervals through the century. Mr (afterwards Sir James) Burrough was a fellow in these days, and was the leading spirit in the work. The college remained untouched until the mastership of the late Dr Guest. Then, in 1854, Salvin built the Hall, whose exterior is as hideous as the interior, with its fine open timber roof, is imposing and beautiful. In 1867 Mr Waterhouse entirely rebuilt Perse's court, and, in the following year, added an apse to the chapel. His court has given a new feature to Cambridge, certainly. But, where colleges are concerned, Mr Waterhouse is not happy, and this huge pile, with its square windows, its pyramidal tower, medallions, and rows of waterspouts, would make a praiseworthy bank or hotel, but, in its present position, is painfully incongruous.

Very shortly after Marie de Valence had founded Pembroke, Edmund Gonville, rector of Terrington St Clement's in Norfolk, founded Gonville Hall for the instruction of twenty scholars in dialect and other sciences. He found a site for his hall in what is now Free School Lane, just behind St Botolph's Church. The foundation took place in 1348, and, during Gonville's lifetime, the name given to the hall was "The Hall of the Annunciation of the Blessed Virgin." But Gonville died in 1351, when his executor, the famous William Bateman, Bishop of Norwich, removed the buildings and placed them opposite his own college of Trinity Hall. Henceforward, the college was known as Gonville Hall, and the old name was retained when Caius re-founded it. The small society—for the college was at first very poor—took possession of its new tenements in 1353, when William de Rougham became master. The previous master of the house in Free School Lane was John Colton, who became Primate of Ireland; and among the masters of Gonville Hall we find the names of John Rickingale, Bishop of Chichester in 1426, and John Skippe, Bishop of Hereford in 1539.

It was during the mastership of Skippe's predecessor, William Bokenham, that John Caius entered the college as an undergraduate. After he had taken his degree he was for a few years Principal of Physwick Hostel, a small house affiliated to Gonville Hall. He left Cambridge, however, about 1540, and travelled to foreign universities, studying medicine at Padua and other academies. He was a man of culture, and his taste was doubtless stimulated by the splendid productions of the Italian Renaissance. We may, in fact, regard him as one of the greatest English humanists, and, like so many of them, as one of the greatest benefactors to his university. On his return to England he practised as a physician, and received the appointment of court physician to Edward VI. and, afterwards, to Queen Mary.

In 1555, he was elected President of the College of Physicians. Having thus risen to considerable eminence, he determined to do something for Gonville Hall. Philip and Mary granted him letters patent in 1557, with which he refounded the college. In this way he gave that impetus to medical study which has since made Caius pre-eminently a doctor's college. His beautiful buildings are sufficient testimony to the elegant taste which he had matured in Italy. Thomas Bacon, master of Gonville Hall and first master of the new foundation, died in 1559, and the society elected Caius to the mastership. At first he was reluctant to accept the dignity, and prevailed so far as to refuse his income as master. His mastership lasted until his death in 1573. He was one of the most disinterested of all Cambridge benefactors, and his learning and talents are beyond praise. One odd feature of his career, which is very characteristic of the uncritical spirit of the time, is his dispute with Dr Key of Oxford as to the relative antiquity of the two universities. To some astonishing legend of Key's, he replied that Cambridge was founded in the year 3538 B.C. by one Cantaber, a Spanish prince, alleging many weighty statements on behalf of his accurate chronology. His *History of Cambridge* contains more trustworthy information than this, but he was singularly prone to the acceptation of spurious etymologies and vain traditions. His contemporaries held him to be something of an atheist, and complained that he showed "a perverse stomach to professors of the gospel." This probably means little more than that he was content with the old religion. He died away from Cambridge, but his body was brought from London to be buried. It was met at Trumpington Ford by the Vice-Chancellor and a procession, who escorted it into Cambridge with almost royal honours.

Among other gifts to the college, Caius left the silver mace encircled with serpents, which is called *Caduceus prudentis gubernatoris*. It was directed to be carried in procession before the master with the *Liber Cognitionis* and the *Pulvinar reverentiae*. There are three portraits of Caius in various parts of the college. That in the Hall, which represents him holding a pink, is the best.

A notable son of Gonville Hall was Sir Thomas Gresham, well known as the founder of the Royal Exchange. He died in 1579, so that he had probably taken his degree before Caius' time. Caius was succeeded in the mastership by Dr Legge, a lawyer and Master in Chancery, who was also Regius Professor of Civil Law. In his day came into residence William Harvey of Folkestone, one of the great glories of the college. His discovery of the circulation of the blood created a revolution in medical science. There are three portraits of Harvey in Caius: one of them, in the Master's Lodge, is attributed to Rembrandt; another in the Combination Room, is a replica of the picture at the Royal College of Physicians. Another great doctor, John Gostlin,* Regius Professor of Physic, became master in 1618. He is said to have objected to the wearing of boots as "more fit for gallants than for civil students." He also gave the Bull Inn, which was his property, to Catharine Hall.

If Caius has its doctors, it has also its prelates. William Linwood, Lord Keeper under Henry VI., and Bishop of St David's in 1442, is commemorated by one of the medallions on the west front. A famous name among others is that of Nicholas Shaxton, Bishop of Salisbury in 1535. The long mastership of Thomas Batchcroft,* who was ejected by the Parliamentary Commissioners and restored in 1660, was distinguished by the residence of Jeremy Taylor. This great divine's father was a barber in Cambridge, and sent his son to Dr Perse's new Free School. Naturally, as a scholar brought up at a school which had been founded from Caius, Taylor became an undergraduate at Caius. He was a precocious theologian, and early attracted the notice of Laud, who transferred him to Oxford and procured him a fellowship at All Souls'. He became Bishop of Down and Connor, and died at Lisburn in 1667. Among theologians his name stands very high, and, as a writer of English, he is in his own style unsurpassed. Cosin also, a no less illustrious example of piety and devout Churchmanship, was bred at Caius, before he became Master of Peterhouse. Both Taylor and Cosin figure in the medallions of the façade. The portrait of Taylor in the Hall is a copy of his picture at All Souls'. There is also a portrait of Cosin painted in 1666. Other prelates of this period are Francis Marsh, Bishop of Limerick and Archbishop of Dublin, Hartstrong, Bishop of Ossory, and Francis White, Bishop, first of Norwich, and then of Ely. To much the same date belongs Judge Jeffreys. A very disreputable undergraduate was Titus Oates, of whom a vehement writer says that he was "a liar from the beginning, cheated his tailor of a gown, which he denied with horrid imprecations." His career at Cambridge had a sudden end, but he managed to obtain a doctor's degree at Salamanca. Thomas Shadwell, who is famous as one of Dryden's *bêtes noires*, was also a member of Caius.

Robert Brady,* Keeper of the Records and Regius Professor of Physic, was master for forty years after Batchcroft's death. He was a supporter of the royal prerogative in its most extreme form, and wrote a History of England to prove his views. Two clergymen were educated at Caius in his time; Prince, who wrote the Worthies of Devon, and Jeremy Collier, the stout antagonist of Restoration drama. Another long mastership was that of Sir Thomas Gooch,* from 1716 to 1754, who, during the same period, was Bishop successively of Bristol, Norwich and Ely. He was succeeded in 1754 by Sir James Burrough, who, for many years before, had interested himself in the architectural condition of Cambridge, and had had a hand in altering almost every college. He was not an unsuccessful architect, although an amateur, but his work is very unequal and it degenerated with the taste of the epoch. Although one of the best known masters, as far as Cambridge is concerned, there is no portrait of him in the college. Another Cambridge architect, William Wilkins, was also a Caius man.

Burrough's successor was Dr John Smith, afterwards Lowndean Professor of Astronomy, who lived till 1795. There is a portrait of him by Reynolds in the Master's Lodge. Later masters have not been so famous. Mr Clark tells us that Dr Benedict Chapman (* Philips) was the last head of a house who rode out in top-boots. Perhaps the name on which Cambridge men will dwell with most affection in connexion with Caius is that of John Hookham Frere, whose translations of Aristophanes have a place in English literature. The mastership of Dr Ferrers,* which began in 1880, has been marked by great progress. The college is no longer exclusively medical, but is winning yearly honours in all the schools, and it has created a good precedent by granting fellowships as a reward of proficiency rather than of mere academic distinction. It has, however, produced, all through its history, great members of every profession. Among its lawyers have been Lord Chancellor Thurlow* and Baron Alderson.* And of its divines, while it reckons the late Dr Harvey Goodwin, Bishop of Carlisle, among the number, the last, but not the least, is the heroic Charles Frederick Mackenzie,* first Bishop of the Universities Mission to Central Africa. Its latest living bishop is Dr Wallis, who was consecrated Bishop of Wellington in New Zealand a year or two ago.

CHAPTER VII

TRINITY HALL

Long the lawyers' college, Trinity Hall maintains a staid legal appearance. Its present arrangement is essentially modern, and the earliest remaining portion is the ivy-covered range of chambers forming the northern side of the Garden Court. This is not earlier than 1560, but, as at Caius, much of the interior work of the main court is original. In the upper storey of this range is the primitive Library, fitted in the sixteenth century with low bookshelves, the tops of which form a double reading desk. This very comfortable arrangement has been followed in the small bookshelves of many of the other libraries. The bulk of the College, including the entrance courts and the small quadrangle, was entirely remodelled in the last century, during the mastership of Sir Nathaniel Lloyd (1710-35) and Sir Edward Simpson (1735-64). The Chapel, south of the large court (an unusual position) belongs to 1729, and the Hall on the west side to 1743. Its interior is very creditable to Georgian taste, although not positively faultless. In 1852, the façade of the college was burned down. The present front is due to Salvin, who built the neighbouring hall of Caius much about the same time. The old gate of the college, which opened into the smaller court, is still commemorated by an opening in the wall, affording a picturesque view of the ivy-covered interior. To a later period belong the new buildings in the Garden Court. The Tutor's House, of white stone, by Mr W. M. Fawcett, is not exactly in harmony with Messrs Grayson & Ould's brick building on the north side, but the latter has been arranged so as to slope obliquely northward, and front the garden; and a too obvious discord has thus been avoided. In itself, this red-brick work, of a Renaissance order, is one of the best things in modern Cambridge, and fulfils, at least from an outside point of view, all the ideal requirements of a collegiate building.

Canon Law, the typical study of the Middle Ages, is the *raison d'être* of Trinity Hall. William Bateman, Bishop of Norwich, founded the College of the Scholars of the Holy Trinity of Norwich in 1350, in order to furnish his diocese with secular priests. His college occupied substantially the same ground as it does to-day. The founder, who also has a claim to be one of the founders of Caius, did not live long to enjoy his work. He was sent by Edward III. on an embassy to Innocent VI., in one of the numerous attempts at arbitration which varied the Hundred Years' War. While engaged in these negotiations the Bishop died. His death was due to the climate of Avignon, which, in that season of plague, was more than ordinarily pestilent. "Avenio ventosa," says the doggrel rhyme, "cum vento fastidiosa, sine vento venenosa." Englishmen, with their usual mistrust of Papal honesty, said that Bateman had been poisoned. He left his foundations of Trinity Hall and the new Gonville Hall in a very incomplete state, and his executor, Archbishop Simon of Sudbury, although he did what he could in the way of building, was too much occupied with his fatal position in the state to attend closely to the condition of the colleges. In fact, Trinity Hall, composed of a master, twenty fellows and three scholars, was very badly off. Early in the fifteenth century they complained to Archbishop Arundel of the insufficiency of their commons, and obtained a dispensation by which they were empowered to add twopence for each weekday and a groat on the Lord's day.

Meanwhile, two of the masters of Trinity Hall are found among the list of bishops. These were the canonists Robert de Stretton, Bishop of Lichfield from 1360 to 1386, and Marmaduke Lumley, Bishop of Lincoln from 1450 to 1452. In the year 1525, Stephen Gardiner* became master. He was a native of Bury St Edmund's and was a fellow of the college. In 1531, he was made Bishop of Winchester, but retained the mastership till his death, esteeming it a refuge to which, in those troublous times, he could always retire. He was, nevertheless, a little out of his reckoning. Although a reformer, he was of the conservative type and was not a *persona grata* to Edward VI., who deprived him of both his mastership and bishoprick. His supplanter at Winchester was John Poynet; at Trinity Hall he was superseded by Walter Haddon, reputed to be the best Latinist of his time. Haddon was Professor of Law and Rhetoric and Public Orator, and, in addition to this, with the assistance of Sir John Cheke, compiled a new code of ecclesiastical law. His reforming activities gained him the Presidency of Magdalen College, Oxford, in 1552, from which he retired at Queen Mary's accession. He died some years later and is buried in Christ Church, Newgate Street.

Mary's reign brought back Gardiner to his college and diocese. Walter Mowse, the second Protestant master, was ousted to make way for the bishop. As Chancellor of England, Gardiner distinguished himself for his reactionary policy, a natural course in one who, having done all he could in the way of reform, knew what gratitude he had to expect from the other side. He died in 1555. There is no doubt that he was an energetic, pushing man who allowed little to stand in his way, and stories were told of how he canvassed for the see of Winchester, doing his best to embitter the last days of Bishop Foxe. He was the bishop who married Philip of Spain to Mary in Winchester Cathedral; and this, with his acts of persecution, have endeared him to the orthodox English historian. But we must make allowance for Protestant hatred, and remember that if such men as Gardiner, Pole, and Gaspar Contarini had lived a century before, we should have been spared the irregularities of the Reformation, while we reaped its advantages. Gardiner's chantry-chapel is well known to all visitors of Winchester Cathedral. There are two portraits of him in Trinity Hall: one in the Combination Room, another in the Master's Lodge. A somewhat less single-minded ecclesiastic was Thomas Thirlby,* fellow of the college, and first and only Bishop of Westminster. He was promoted in 1550 to Norwich, and to Ely in 1554, when he, too, gained some reputation as a persecutor of the new religion. Richard Sampson, Bishop of Lichfield, belongs also to this period.

Henry Hervey, who followed Gardiner, was a great builder, and we owe the Library to him. From his time onward the college was the legal centre of Cambridge, and helped to raise English law to a position which fully realised Bateman's desire that England should not be "out-lawed" by other countries. As Canon Law became superseded by Civil Law, the original purpose of the college and its connexion with Norwich were quite forgotten. John Cowell, master from 1598 to 1611, was a great foe, however, to Sir Edward Coke and the common lawyers. His book on the King's Prerogative was burned by order of the House of Commons. Another legal worthy of the time was Sir Robert Naunton, Public Orator, and author of *Fragmenta Regalia,* who had also some connexion with Trinity College. He is memorable for an insulting remark which he made to the Spanish Ambassador, Gondomar, on account of which he was kept a close prisoner in his own house, stoutly refusing to apologise.

The Regius Professorship of Civil Law became the practical monopoly of Trinity Hall in 1666, when Dr John Clark was elected to the office. It was only on the election of the present Professor Clark that the succession was broken. Of these professors, one, Dr George Oxenden, held the mastership and professorship together. Meanwhile, we find one or two bishops, notably William Barlow, Bishop of Lincoln from 1608 to 1614, whose name is familiar to controversialists on the subject of Anglican Orders. The beginning of the eighteenth century produced two more, Adam Otley, Bishop of St David's and Richard Reynolds, Bishop of Lincoln. About the same time, Trinity Hall had the honour of educating Philip Dormer Stanhope, fourth Earl of Chesterfield (* W. Hoare). It would be interesting to know more about the life of this celebrated gentleman at Cambridge, but he doubtless employed his time in picking up miscellaneous knowledge and laying the foundations of his delightful style. I forgot to mention that another famous nobleman was a Trinity Hall man—Lord Howard of Effingham, who commanded the English fleet against the Spanish Armada. In Nathaniel, Lord Crewe,* Bishop of Durham, the college produced a devout prelate and Jacobite. He died in his ninetieth year (1633).

Lawyers of the eighteenth century are absolutely innumerable. Sir Nathaniel Lloyd,* master from 1710 to 1735, was King's Advocate; his successor, Sir Edward Simpson,* was Dean of Arches. Sir John Eardley Wilmot,* Lord Chief Justice of England, was another noted member of the college. His life nearly spans the last century. Dr John Andrews,* Master of Faculties, dying in 1747, left the College £20,000, which was to be paid after the death of his two sisters and expended in building new wings to the river. Dr Samuel Halifax,* Professor of Law from 1770 to 1782, was clergyman as well as lawyer. Previously, he had held for two years the two University Professorships of Arabic. His elevation to the see of Gloucester in 1781 was a suitable reward of such versatility. He was followed in his Professorship by Dr Joseph Jowett, who made a garden out of the strip of ground at the angle formed by the outer walls of the old court and of the principal quadrangle. It faced the lane east of the cottage, and excited some ridicule. Archdeacon Wrangham's epigram has been often quoted:

A little garden little Jowett made
And fenced it with a little palisade;
But when this little garden made a little talk,
He changed it to a little gravel walk.
If you would know the mind of little Jowett,
This little garden don't a little show it.

The list of legal celebrities in the last century is also adorned by the name of Lord Mansfield, whose bust, by Nollekens, is in the Hall.

We now come to the present century. Sir Alexander Cockburn (* Watts), Lord Chief Justice, was a member of the college during the earlier half, and the name of Sir Herbert Jenner Fust, master from 1843 to 1852, is also well known. Sir Henry Maine's reputation is European. This great historian, lawyer and philosopher, occupied the chair of Civil Law from 1847 to 1854. When, in 1877, Dr Geldart died, he was elected Master, and died in 1888. During the last year of his life, he was Whewell Professor of International Law. There is a portrait of him in the Hall, by Lowes Dickinson. Needless to say, Trinity Hall is represented on the Bench of to-day, and the Lodge contains two portraits (by Dickinson) of Mr Justice Romer.

Literature pure and simple has never been well represented at "the Hall." Thomas Tusser was educated here, but a great gap exists between the old-fashioned bucolic poet and the next writer. The name of Sir Edward Bulwer-Lytton (* copy from Maclise) is, however, not inconsiderable. His part in nineteenth-century literature may be very largely ascribed to his Cambridge associations and friendships. And the growth of an essentially modern science has been stimulated by another Trinity Hall man, Henry Fawcett (* Rathbone), Postmaster General and Professor of Political Economy from 1863 to 1884. There is another portrait of him, by Professor Herkomer, in the Fitzwilliam Museum. And, speaking of the Fitzwilliam Museum, it must not be forgotten that the peer to whom that institution owes its foundation came from Trinity Hall also.

To the modern undergraduate Trinity Hall is known chiefly as the head of the river, a position which, until the present year, has been for some time its monopoly. However, it is also well known in the schools, and not only in the school of law. Under Dr Latham (* Holl and Dickinson) the college has increased in popularity, and, both in size and importance, has attained a place in the first rank of colleges.

CHAPTER VIII

CORPUS CHRISTI COLLEGE

One of the prettiest spots in the whole University is the tiny medieval court on the north side of Corpus. You have only to turn your back on the ugly Hall, and look at three sides of a venerable, low quadrangle clothed with ivy and stained with age, and you can imagine yourself back in the days of the Edwards, when the pious members of the Cambridge benefit societies founded the college. Times have changed, and the court has been repaired fairly often; but the place retains its medieval flavour. There is still the gallery which communicated between the college and St Bene't's Church, while St Bene't's was the college chapel; with the aid of a key, you may go straight from under the roof of Corpus into church, without leaving cover. And, in one corner of the court, the kitchen, with its great spit revolving in the draught, is a continual source of interest to all visitors. However, medieval Corpus was never very conspicuous, and, like most things medieval, it grew incommodious. Mr William Wilkins, an architect of some knowledge, who had taken his degree at Caius, was selected in 1823 to renew Corpus in the Gothic taste, then becoming fashionable. His design, which he executed between 1823 and 1827, was highly praised, and during the next ten years he left some notable marks of his hand in Cambridge. The great court of Corpus is a singular instance of the fluctuation of taste. What was then considered handsome—it was certainly audacious—is to-day an eye-sore. The proportions of the great court are noble, and everything is conceived on a grand scale. The Hall and Library are both fine apartments, and the Chapel is commanding; but the whole building is shallow, and its detail is flimsy and jejune. All Wilkins' work, here, at King's and at Trinity, deserves careful study; for it shows how the architects of the first half of the century, with the experience of past ages at their command, failed even in the elementary matter of imitation.

Corpus has the singular distinction of having been founded by a Gild. The Gild or Benefit Society was an important institution in medieval Cambridge, and each church had one attached to it. Somewhere towards the end of the thirteenth century, when the festival of Corpus Christi was become a recognised feast of the Church, a society of this kind was founded in the parish of St Bene't, and took the title of Corpus Christi in honour of the Blessed Sacrament. What induced the corporation to found a college is unknown; its action is at all events a testimony to the love of learning which was spreading at this time among the middle classes. In 1352, it obtained a charter from Edward III. for the foundation of a college.

The alderman of the Gild at this date was Henry, Duke of Lancaster, cousin to the King. One gild, however, was not sufficient to carry out the work of itself, and the Gild of Corpus Christi achieved its desire by uniting itself with the Gild of Our Lady, which was connected with St Mary's by the Market, the present University Church. To this union the College owes its coat of arms. In two out of the four quarters we see the "pelican in her piety," the emblem of the Blessed Sacrament; in the other two are the lilies emblematic of the Blessed Virgin Mary. Another interesting person connected with the foundation is John Goldcorne, an ex-alderman of the Gild of Corpus Christi. He had generously given some of his property to Bishop Bateman when the bishop removed Caius College to its present site. He gave Corpus the fine drinking-horn which still is the chief piece of plate in the rich collection belonging to the house. It was probably the horn used at feasts of the Gild; it is one of the best specimens of the kind in existence.

Thomas of Eltisley, a village between Cambridge and St Neots, was the first master. Like most other colleges, its medieval history is not very extraordinary. Like most other colleges, too, its scholars "kept" their chapels in a parish church, the adjacent church of St Bene't. College and church have always been closely connected, and even to-day, when the college has ceased to bear its familiar name of Bene't College, the advowson of St Bene't's is in its gift. In process of time, it built the south chancel aisle, which it reserved for itself. This was divided into two stories, an upper and an under, and was entered from the gallery which still exists between the church and the old court. Finally, in the sixteenth century, Sir Nicholas Bacon,* the famous Lord Keeper, who had been educated at Corpus, gave the structure of a chapel. This was built almost on the site of the present one. It is characteristic of the age that, to build this chapel, stone was taken from the dissolved abbey of Thorney and from Barnwell Priory.

Matthew Parker, master from 1544 to 1553, was the great ornament of the college at this period. He is more famous as Archbishop of Canterbury than as a don, but Corpus holds his name in great honour. His great collection of manuscripts is preserved in the Library. The bequest was accompanied by one of those odd provisions by which benefactors ensured the jealous care of their possessions after their death. If twenty-five manuscripts are lost, the collection is to go to Caius; if Caius is guilty of neglect, it passes to Trinity Hall. The provision is rigidly attended to, and the inspection of the manuscripts is an affair of great circumstance, for which the presence of the librarian, a fellow and a scholar is necessary. Perhaps the most historical document in the Library is the original draft of the Thirty-Nine Articles. Parker also left some very valuable plate to the college, cups and apostle-spoons. There is a portrait of him in the Hall, and another in the Master's Lodge.

Corpus has a distinguished roll of Elizabethan worthies. Besides Sir Nicholas Bacon and Parker, we find the names of two dramatists, Christopher Marlowe, one of the greatest of all, and Giles Fletcher, the collaborator of Beaumont. The father of the latter was also a member of the college, and became Bishop, first of Bristol, then of London. George Wishart, the Scottish martyr, was here at some time early in the sixteenth century. In 1590 John Jegon* became master. Afterwards, as Bishop of Norwich, Jegon was not a great success: as Master of Corpus his strictness made him unpopular. There is a story that he fined some of the scholars for a breach of rules, and applied the proceeds to the repair of the college. One of the delinquents afterwards wrote on a wall of the college this couplet,

> Dr Jegon, Bene't College Master,
> Broke the scholars' heads and gave the wall a plaster.

Beneath this elegant conceit Jegon wrote a distich of his own.

> Knew I but the wag that wrote this verse in bravery,
> I'd commend him for his wit, but whip him for his knavery.

Jegon was Vice-Chancellor from 1596 to 1601, and his arms appear on the plaster ceiling of the old Senate House, now incorporated in the University Library. His brother Thomas succeeded him at Corpus and was also Vice-Chancellor in 1609. Both brothers died in 1618.

During the Commonwealth Richard Love* was Master, and was also Dean of Ely as long as deaneries were suffered to exist. At the Restoration, Peter Gunning became master for a year, and then passed to St John's. Gunning's part in Church History is well known, and his short residence may be esteemed an honourable item in the history of the college. Seven years after his time, another scholar of repute became master, John Spencer (* Van der Myn), Dean of Ely, and author of a book *De Legibus Hebraeorum*. Corpus has always been rich in ecclesiastics. It produced a second Archbishop of Canterbury in Thomas Tenison* who is famous for his interest in education and his benefactions to schools. In the next generation another Primate, Thomas Herring,* came from Corpus. An Archbishop of York belonging to the foundation was Richard Sterne, afterwards Master of Jesus and grandfather of the great sentimentalist. Matthias Mawson,* master from 1724 to 1744, was elevated in 1740 to the Bishopric of Chichester and translated in 1754 to Ely. On the other hand, Samuel Wesley was also at Corpus, so that modern Methodism, the creation of his famous sons, may look with reverence upon the college.

The Master's Lodge contains a very complete series of portraits, but the later masters are none of them very noticeable. It cannot be said that the heads of houses during the early part of the present century were interesting beings, although they themselves were not without positive convictions on the point. Dr John Lamb (* Sir W. Beechey), was master from 1822 to 1850, and supplemented his office with the Deanery of Bristol. His mastership was signalised by the entire rebuilding of the college under William Wilkins. Whether the copy of Raffaelle's School of Athens (attributed to Poussin) which this radical builder presented to the college is sufficient compensation for the damage inflicted in a matter of doubt. The present buildings have nourished some excellent scholars. Of living celebrities the three brothers Perowne may be mentioned—Bishop, Master, and Archdeacon. The portrait of Dr E. H. Perowne in the Hall is by Rudolph Lehmann; that of his brother, the Bishop of Worcester, is by the Hon. John Collier. The late librarian, Samuel S. Lewis (* Brock) was a world-wide authority on gems. His collection, containing many of the finest engraved gems existing, now belongs to the college, forming a treasure little inferior to Archbishop Parker's manuscripts. And, turning to the religious memories of Corpus, no one who appreciates a life of entire self-sacrifice and devotion will fail to pay a tribute to the portrait of Thomas Ragland, Fellow of the College, and missionary to Tinnevelly. It will be seen that the history of Corpus is throughout almost entirely ecclesiastical, and it is still a favourite college for undergraduates who wish to proceed to Holy Orders. Among its latest honours has been the elevation of its librarian, Dr Harmer, to the Bishoprick of Adelaide. Although one of the smaller foundations, its priceless collections give Corpus an importance second to that of very few colleges, while the unique history of its foundation singles it out from the rest.

CHAPTER IX

KING'S COLLEGE

Henry VI. is the most famous of the founders of colleges in Cambridge, but his plan has been adhered to least of all. King's has gone through several vicissitudes. The magnificent chapel stood south, not north, of the original college. That college was to have consisted of four courts; the fourth was to be on the other side of the river, and a covered bridge was to lead to it, as to the present fourth court of St John's. As at Wykeham's Oxford College, with which King's has so many points of resemblance, the west end of the chapel was to be supplemented with cloisters and an ample tower. Only one court was built, which now is part of the University Library. The college has been transferred to the other side of the chapel, and consists of a scattered series of more or less modern buildings. From some points of view, the change is to be regretted, but, had it not been made, we should have lost the unique view of King's and Clare from the Backs, which disputes the honours of Cambridge with the Trinity lime walk.

King's Chapel was very nearly a century in building. Henry VI. laid its foundation stone on July 25th, 1446, and the workmen continued at it till 1479 or thereabout. Edward IV. gave £1000 towards it, but the works lay idle till 1508, when Henry VII. came forward with £5000. Another £5000 was paid over by his executors in 1513, and in 1515 the chapel stood for the first time as it stands now. The stained glass was added under two contracts, one bearing date 1516, the second 1526. In 1536 the screen and most of the stalls were added, and in 1774 Essex spoiled the east end with some inferior Gothic wood carving, which, fortunately, has lately been removed.

King's College

King's College Chapel

This is the history of the main fabric. As a building, its faults are shared in common by all its contemporaries. It is possible to accuse King's Chapel of monotony, and it must be confessed that its constant repetition of the same ornaments all over its surface shows a lack of invention. But it may be said without any doubt that no building raised in Europe after 1500 is so pure a specimen of Gothic as this; and, with all its faults, and especially its strong tendency to mere bigness, it stands first in beauty among those of our churches which are not cathedrals—that is, after Westminster Abbey. The exterior, with its corner turrets, its row of tall windows, its flanking chantries and its immense buttresses, is simple in design and gorgeous in execution. The north and south porches, which are exceptionally good for their date, afford a certain relief from the general sameness. Internally, the charm of the general effect is extraordinary, and every Cambridge man must have felt it at some time or other. Its length is 316 feet, its breadth 45½ feet, its height 78 feet; and this vast area is flooded with the exquisite colours of the stained windows. Even the roof, an unbroken expanse of that development of vaulting known as fan tracery, must give the palm to the windows. Without its stained glass, King's Chapel would be, like the Lady Chapel at Ely, merely an interesting relic. As it is, it is the rival of Fairford as the possessor of the most complete set of windows of the Renaissance period in England. Indeed, it would be difficult to find their parallel anywhere. Troyes is full of glass of the period, and, intrinsically, the windows of one of its churches, St Martin-ès-Vignes, are of equal interest, although much later. For depth of colour and systematic treatment these cannot be matched. They form a connected exposition of the Gospel History, proceeding by type and antitype from the conception of the Blessed Virgin, through the life of Our Lord and the apostolic history to the Virgin's death. In each window there is an isolated figure or "messenger" between the compartments, who bears a scroll with an appropriate Latin text. Thus the windows embodied the whole plan of salvation, showing the type, the prophecy and the fulfilment. They culminate, in the east window, in the central fact of the Crucifixion. The west window, representing, in accordance with general custom, the Last Judgment, is modern (Clayton and Bell) and is in very fair, although far from complete harmony with the older glass. The merit of the latter is not sustained all through, and the windows on the south side, nearest the altar, are coarsely treated in comparison with the rest.[3] Mr C. E. Kempe is at present restoring the windows dealing with the lives of Joachim, Anna, and the Blessed Virgin, which suffered from the enemies of so-called popery.

There are a thousand things to notice other than the windows. I have mentioned the roof. To understand its construction it is necessary to pay a visit to the space between the roofs, where the whole skeleton of the vaulting is to be seen and its wonderful engineering appreciated. The woodwork of the chapel is good, especially the screen, a very fine and graceful example of that Italian style which filtered into England through the court of Francis I. It bears the love-knot and twisted initials of Henry VIII. and Anne Boleyn. The organ-case upon it belongs to 1606; the organ itself was built eighty years later by Renatus Harris, but has been almost entirely renewed since. The canopies of the choir-stalls are only a little old-

[3] Much of the glass was re-touched in the last century, and some was added about 1845.

er than the organ, and look best at a distance. Then there is the stone-carving in the antechapel, where the great coats-of-arms and supporters, the rose and portcullis of Henry VII. are repeated over and over again. Lastly, in the series of chantries there are one or two interesting brasses. Provost Hacombleyn's chantry, on the south side, commemorates the provost who gave the beautiful lectern. He died in 1528, and is buried here. The window contains some good old glass; a portrait of Henry VI. and two pictures of Our Lady and St Nicholas of Myra, who are the patrons of the chapel. In the centre of the chantry is the altar tomb of Lord Blandford, only son of the great Duke of Marlborough. He died here in 1703.

For two hundred years after the completion of the chapel, the old northern court sufficed. To the south of the chapel was the Provost's Lodge, which stood against the last bay, and, with other college buildings, bordered the western side of King's Parade. In 1724 James Gibbs began the present buildings with his beautiful classical pile, which runs at right angles to the chapel from near its south-west corner. Fellows' Building is in Gibbs' best manner. It is an extremely plain building, with a rusticated basement and a great central opening, which runs through the first two stories and cuts into the third. This may be thought an unnecessary intrusion, but Gibbs had dispensed with an order throughout the building, and some relief was imperative. At any rate, the chief defect of this part of King's is its hideous chimney-stacks, which are only too visible from the street.

Just a century later William Wilkins, who was rearing marvellous edifices in the Gothic mode, was let loose on King's. He began with the space opposite the chapel, and built the long row which includes the Hall, Combination Room, Library, Provost's Lodge, and several sets of rooms. This row begins at King's Parade and continues past the southern end of Gibbs' Building to within a short distance of the river—nearly 200 yards of supremely bad imitation Gothic. In this range of buildings the Hall is the only one which attracts much attention. It is large and gloomy, with a gallery at each end, and an elaborate plaster roof copied from Crosby Hall. Sir Robert Walpole has the place of honour above the high table, but there are very few portraits, and the best is that of the late Henry Bradshaw, University Librarian. Wilkins was not satisfied with his undertaking. In 1828 he proceeded to lay King's open to the road. The old Lodge was taken down, and a Gothic screen thrown across from the New Building to the south-east corner of the chapel. In the middle of this is the gateway, famous under many nicknames. To say that this fanciful structure is ugly is not strictly true: it has a very distinguished air about it, but it belongs decidedly to the era of the Brighton Pavilion. It would be appropriate in any country but England, and under any other name but Gothic.

Sir Gilbert Scott added the small court known as Chetwynd Court some forty years later. Its eastern side follows King's Parade in a line with the end of Wilkins' Building, and the face opposite Free School Lane is adorned with a statue of Henry VIII. Scott was too conservative and kept to Wilkins' style too much; the result is not very successful. It was reserved for Mr G. F. Bodley to build the beautiful river court, which was completed on two sides in 1893. Bodley's Building is the architectural success of Cambridge in the present century, and compares very well with the same artist's court at Magdalen College, Oxford. Its style is late fifteenth century: it consists of a ground-floor, two stories, and a gabled attic. The corner-staircase and the oriel of the south side are the chief features, for the use of ornament is very sparing. The rose and portcullis are introduced in places, and on the western end, which drops into the river, are carved the arms of Eton, King's, and the tutelary see of Lincoln.

The only other buildings which remain to be mentioned are the last-century bridge, crossing the river by a single span, and the choir-school, a very handsome red-brick building in the meadows west of the college. It deserves notice as one of the very few really pretty dwelling-houses round Cambridge, and as an integral part of this noble and unique foundation.

In examining the motives which led to the foundation of the various colleges, it is interesting to observe how many of them were suggested by similar and almost contemporary foundations at Oxford. One may safely say that the boundary-line between the middle ages and the new learning of the Renaissance was crossed when William of Wykeham founded his colleges of St Mary at Winchester and Oxford. The political importance of William of Wykeham and of his successors in the see of Winchester made their work very conspicuous: two of them, William of Waynflete and Richard Foxe, during their tenure of the see, proved no less munificent benefactors to Oxford than Wykeham had been. The connection of the see of Winchester with the Renaissance forced itself upon everybody's attention. Henry VI. was especially impressed with it. Two bishops, Cardinal Beaufort and Waynflete, played a prominent part at his court; and it is to the latter that we doubtless owe many hints for the foundation of King's College. However, at first, Henry VI. undertook the work without any idea of uniting it with his school at Eton. The college which he incorporated in 1440 was a very humble affair. It was restricted to a master and twelve scholars, and the space chosen for it was small and inconvenient. One of the main arteries of Cambridge ran west of it; the whole site of the present buildings was blocked up with houses; the form of the court had to be adapted to its narrow and cramped position. But, two years later, the king's plans matured. His foundation of 1443 took a much larger form. It converted King's into a finishing-school, as it were, for his Highness' poor scholars of Eton. The dedication of the college was changed. Hitherto, in reference to the saint who presided over Henry's birthday, it had been called the King's College of St Nicholas. It now added St Mary, the patroness of Eton, to its title. Thus it became an exact counterpart of New College at Oxford. Although Henry projected his buildings on a far more magnificent scale than anything of which Wykeham had dreamed, they had nevertheless a certain resemblance to the Oxford buildings. The plan includes a great tower and a cloister west of it, such as were built at Oxford. On the whole, the Founder must have been thinking very closely of the colleges at Winchester and Oxford, when he set his hand to this splendid work. He made Waynflete, then Warden of Winchester, Provost of Eton; and Waynflete was the guiding spirit of the charter by which the two communities were regulated.[4]

[4] Waynflete had, no doubt, something to say about the building of the College. He was a great architect, as his work at Tattershall Castle shows.

The first provost of King's came from the opposite side of the street. His name was William Millington, a fellow of Clare. We are told that he was "set back for factious favouring of Yorkshiremen." At any rate, Waynflete probably held the reins of both foundations until his translation to Winchester, which took place in 1447. Among the earliest members of the college are one or two famous names. Nicholas Close or Cloose, Bishop, first of Carlisle and afterwards of Lichfield, was certainly the overseer of the new chapel and perhaps its architect. Thomas Rotherham, whose name is so closely connected with the history of both universities, was fellow of King's, and gave £140 to the chapel. His portrait is in the Hall. Rather younger than these was Oliver King, Bishop of Exeter, who afterwards distinguished himself as Bishop of Bath and Wells. The immense Perpendicular building of Bath Abbey, which is due to his energy, is clearly suggested by King's Chapel, and reproduces many of its details. John Chedworth, who is actually the first provost of the new foundation, became Bishop of Lincoln. His successor, Robert Woodlark, was the founder of St Catharine's College. Another remarkable man of the end of the fifteenth century was Nicholas West, whose conduct as fellow was extremely indecorous. His temper was naturally hasty, and, when he was defeated in his candidature for a proctorship, he made an attempt to set the Provost's Lodge on fire. Being baulked in this endeavour, he ran off with the college spoons. What action the college took is not recorded, but we are informed that, after this ebullition of temper, the quarrelsome fellow "became a new man, D.D., and Bishop of Ely." Not only did he combine these three attributes, but, in penitence for his wild design on the Provost's Lodge, built part of it. This was, of course, the old Provost's Lodge, south-east of the chapel.

Penitence, too, moved Henry VII. to finish the chapel. As a member of the House of Lancaster, his hereditary duty compelled him to complete a work which even Edward IV. had found pleasure in favouring; while, as one of the most extortionate and unjust kings who were establishing their thrones about that time, his conscience invited him to do something as an *amende honorable* for his misdeeds. King's College was already looked upon as a royal legacy, and all the kings in their turn were well disposed to it, but none promoted its welfare so much as Henry VII., although his benefits were chiefly posthumous. The provost to whom the task fell of seeing that Henry's bequests were rightly fulfilled was Robert Hacombleyn, who also had a reputation in his time as a commentator on Aristotle. He lies buried in one of the chantries south of the antechapel. He was succeeded by Edward Fox, a native of Gloucestershire, who was provost from 1528 to 1538. Fox was a reformer, but it is said of him that he had "prudence to avoid persecution." He was essentially a diplomatist, and held the Bishopric of Hereford during the last three years of his provostship. He was busily engaged by Henry VIII. in the matter of the divorce, and was sent to Clement VII., Stephen Gardiner being his companion. Afterwards he was ambassador to France and Germany, and finally to the Schmalkaldic League, when Henry, in his new-fangled zeal for the Reformation, felt disposed to join that body. At King's he was followed by George Day, who filled the office till 1548, and held the see of Chichester with it.

Henry VIII. was a benefactor to King's as well as his father. He had other foundations of his own to look after, however, and seems to have regarded King's as a good recruiting-ground for Christ Church at Oxford—the college whose glory really belongs to Wolsey. Among those students of Eton and King's whom we find thus transferred is Robert Aldrich. Aldrich has not much to do with King's, but was Master, Fellow, and finally Provost of Eton, and, after several promotions, became Bishop of Carlisle, where he remained until 1556, having successfully weathered all the religious storms of his age. Another very prominent member of the college was Richard Cox, fellow in 1519. His strong Lutheran opinions brought him into favour after the divorce. He had been a Canon of Wolsey's original Cardinal College; in 1546 he was made Dean of Christ Church. He was also tutor to Edward VI. As a commissioner at Oxford, he displayed great fury against the papists, and, at Mary's accession, not unnaturally fled to Strasburg, where he had the congenial society of Peter Martyr Vermigli. As Bishop of Ely from 1559 to 1582, he had time to modify his opinions, and it is recorded of him that he hated puritans as much as papists. Queen Elizabeth is said to have disliked him; he must certainly have been very far from her mind.

To the names of these ecclesiastics we may add that of Edward Hall, fellow of King's, who claimed direct descent from Albert II. of Austria, and retired to Oxford. Richard Croke was a learned Grecian of King's, who went to Oxford in order to be near Grocyn. He found patrons in the munificent Warham and Sir Thomas More, and was one of that *coterie* which included Colet and Erasmus. After he had travelled abroad and lectured in Greek at Leipsic and Louvain, he returned to England and became Professor of Greek at Cambridge. This was in 1522. Later on, he was engaged in the divorce, acting as Counsel to the Italian Universities, and was made a Canon of Christ Church in 1532. He died in 1588 as Rector of Long Buckby. Yet another of his class was Dr Richard Mulcaster, who, at a somewhat later period, transferred his talent and vast learning to Oxford, and finally became famous as Master of Merchant Taylors' School.

Very seldom has royalty appeared at Cambridge with such magnificence as on the occasion of Elizabeth's visit in 1564. Although her actual abode was at Queens' College, she spent most of her time in King's Chapel. The provost at this time was Dr Philip Baker, who had succeeded Dr Brassie in 1558. Elizabeth was in her element: she was in a seat of learning, and wanted to show herself as profound as any of them. She rode to hear Te Deum and evensong at King's, dressed in the most gorgeous apparel which even she could assume. At the door the public orator praised her in long-winded Latin. When his compliments tended to the fulsome, she said "*Non est veritas*," when they passed probability, she said "*Utinam!*" Next day was Sunday, and the politic Chancellor, Andrew Perne of Peterhouse, who had burned corpses to please her sister, made a Latin sermon before her on the text "Let every soul be subject unto the higher powers"—a command which he himself had obeyed to the letter. The Queen was highly pleased. Indeed, most of her visit was occupied in hearing Latin disputations, and nothing delighted her so much as the Latin of Matthew Hutton, who laid the foundation of his fortune by this means. On the Sunday, after Dr Perne's sermon, she again attended King's Chapel for evensong; and, in the evening, having performed her religious duties so well, the Virgin Queen once more returned to the antechapel and witnessed the *Aulularia* of Plautus. This must have vexed the good puritans of the day! It is necessary to remark that the use of college chapels for dramatic purposes was very common, and nothing was thought of it. The Commencements in Great St Mary's were infinitely more impious ceremonies. Even now, when a mastership falls vacant, many college chapels are used for the conclave of fellows, as the chapel ensures more privacy than any other part of the buildings.

Dr Philip Baker, who took part in these solemn revels, was succeeded in 1569 by Dr Roger Goade, a very serious divine. His son was present at the Synod of Dort, a fact indicative of the family's opinions. King's produced, indeed, during the Tudor period, a large number of grave and weighty persons. Sir John Cheke had been provost during the reign of Edward VI., and, together with the violently Protestant Walter Haddon, then fellow, and afterwards Master of Trinity Hall, had done important work as an ecclesiastical lawyer. Then there was Giles Fletcher, brother of the Bishop of London and uncle of the dramatist. This remarkable man was Ambassador to the Court of Muscovy in 1588, and concluded a treaty of commerce with Ivan the Terrible. His book "Of the Russe Commonwealthe" has been an indispensable authority for all subsequent historians of Russia. He was made Treasurer of St Paul's in 1597. A more famous name still is that of Sir Francis Walsingham, the great minister of Elizabeth. He was a fellow commoner and left many valuable books to the library. Dr Thomas Wylson, fellow of the college, was also a well-known politician of the same reign. He was tutor to Elizabeth's cousins, the young Brandons, Dukes of Suffolk, and was ambassador to Holland in 1576. In 1577, he became Secretary of State, and, in 1579 Dean of Durham. It is said of him that he was "master of every subject." His correspondence forms part of the Harleian MSS.

At Dr Goade's death, in 1610, we approach dangerous times. Dr Benjamin Whichcot, a liberal puritan, became master in 1644. It is generally supposed that his friendship with the Earl of Manchester, who occupied Cambridge for the Parliament, was the salvation of the stained glass in the chapel. He was far too learned a man to be bigoted, and was more of the type of Milton than of the ordinary puritan divine. Dr Whichcot was a classic, and advised young preachers to imitate Demosthenes and Cicero. The gentle and metaphysical Cudworth was his friend, and he died at Cudworth's house in 1683, having been dispossessed of the provostship since 1660. His memory was held long afterwards in great esteem, and a selection from his discourses was edited by the third Lord Shaftesbury, the pupil of John Locke and author of the *Characteristics*.

Of a very opposite type to Dr Whichcot was the mathematician William Oughtred, author of a book called *Clavis Mathematica*, and an adept in archery. One writer says of him that "Mathematics were not only recreation to him, but Epicurism." In spite of this devotion to abstract sciences, he was an ardent royalist, and, on hearing of the Restoration, died of joy. Edmund Waller, the poet, was also at King's about the same time. We may imagine that his ecstasy at the Restoration took a more substantial form. Another type of don altogether is shown us in Dr William Gage, who attended chapel without a break for nine years, and read fifteen chapters of Holy Scripture every day of his life. This exemplary gentleman received the living of St Anne, Blackfriars, where he died in 1653.

After the Restoration, the list of provosts becomes uninteresting, and the college history becomes a very ordinary record. The privileges of the foundation were strengthened with age. It was very conservative and adhered very closely to the Founder's plan, while other colleges were opening their doors more widely and competition was becoming a recognised part of university life. It was autonomous: its members did not proceed to public examinations in the schools, but gained their degree by an examination of their own. An Eton Foundation Scholarship was the almost inevitable prelude to a scholarship and finally a fellowship at King's. Under such circumstances the history of a college, however sound its scholarship, is likely to be rather quiet. In other respects, too, the existence of King's has been isolated. Its visitor is the Bishop of Lincoln, and the college is a peculiar in the diocese of Lincoln. It also enjoyed the unique privilege of being exempt from proctorial jurisdiction, and many a refugee from the proctor's mild justice has sought sanctuary in King's without fear of extradition treaties.

It is not, however, to be supposed that this noble college was at any time without its worthies. Sir William Temple was educated here. Although his name is doubtless an ornament to the college, he must have been an insufferable thorn in the side of his pastors and masters, for he was the last man in the world to have an ill conceit of himself. Two more genial names appear later. In the absence of a portrait of the Founder, a painting of Sir Robert Walpole hangs at the end of the hall. He was always a loving son of the college, and his son, the even more famous Horace,* was here as well. Charles Pratt, Earl Camden* and Lord Chancellor of England, is another name connected with the college; and Townshend, a third statesman of the Georgian era, was likewise brought up at Eton and King's. To turn aside from politics to the path of pure learning, we find a very prodigy in the person of Thomas Hyde, afterwards Archdeacon of Gloucester. At the age of eighteen he performed the almost incredible task, which till then had been deemed impossible, of transcribing the Persian Pentateuch out of its Hebrew characters. It is scarcely surprising to find that this precocious divine did not shine in ordinary conversation. But his learning met its recompense in a Canonry at Christ Church, and Hebraists of his own age did not scruple to reckon him equal as an Orientalist to Bochert and Pococke.

The name of Sumner occurs twice in the list of provosts, once in 1756 and again in 1797, and, among others of the name, John Bird Sumner,* the famous Archbishop of Canterbury, was a King's man. Earlier in the century lived the painfully erudite William Coxe,* who, as Archdeacon of Wiltshire, devoted his attention to the Duke of Marlborough and the Hapsburg family. His researches, although their method is antiquated and their style is hopelessly dull, are yet invaluable to the student, and his name is not by any means the least among those of the historians whom Cambridge has produced. But to the majority of persons, the ecclesiastical celebrities of King's are overshadowed by the fame of Charles Simeon, who was a fellow of the college for considerably more than half a century and, during that time, was a parish priest of the town. He was the chief of those men who roused the Church of England from her last-century apathy and revived her ancient fervour. Although his position was, owing to circumstances, somewhat more restricted, he was to Cambridge of his day what Cosin and Andrewes had been to the Cambridge of theirs, and the influence which he exercised from Cambridge over the length and breadth of England was almost unbounded. He is buried in the antechapel of King's beneath a stone on which his initials are engraved, and there is a bust of him in the University Library. The traditions which he left to King's have never been entirely lost. The Church of England has had few more devoted sons than the late George Williams, who, as fellow of King's, advocated warmly the establishment of friendly relations with the churches of the East. Older members of the university still remember him as "Jerusalem" Williams. And, although his life was very retired and he was seldom absent for any length of time from Cambridge, the late William Ralph Churton, Canon of St Alban's, was for the last forty years of his life probably the most active of all the English clergy in promoting missionary work and extending the Church in the colonies.

In mentioning these names, there are others which have been necessarily omitted. The episcopal list of the college is a long one, and includes, among many more prelates, the famous names of Edmund Gheast, Bishop of Rochester and Jewel's successor at Salisbury; William Wickham, Bishop of Lincoln and afterwards the second Bishop of that name at Winchester; and John Pearson, Bishop of Chester, who, first a fellow here, was subsequently Master of Trinity. Among noblemen, the great ambassador, Stratford Canning, afterwards Lord Stratford de Redcliffe (* Herkomer), occupies a conspicuous place. Among ordinary laymen, we find Roger Lupton, a Jacobean worthy, founder of Sedbergh School; and, much later, the poet, Thomas Lisle Bowles. In the antechapel, a plain stone covers the remains of Dr Richard Okes, provost from 1850 to 1889. And close by, under a similar stone, is buried Henry Bradshaw (* Herkomer), University Librarian, one of the finest scholars of the century, who opened a new epoch in the history of liturgical study. By the side of the south door will be found a tablet in memory of the late James Kenneth Stephen, an incomparable orator, whose little volumes of verse proved him the successor of Calverley among Cambridge poets.

Within the last twenty years the college has undergone a complete change. It is no longer the exclusively Etonian college which it was. Its scholarships, with the exception of a very few, have been thrown open to all competitors, and the large majority of undergraduates now at King's have never been at Eton. Although, from the standpoint of the lover of antiquity, this departure from the Founder's scheme is to be seriously regretted, yet it cannot but be admitted that, in the present century, the exclusive scheme is impracticable, and newer methods have to be followed. At all events, the plan works very well, and in no generation is King's likely to lose its prestige, nor is that *esprit de corps* which "Henry's holy shade" seems to inspire, at all likely to diminish.

CHAPTER X

QUEENS' COLLEGE

Queens' disputes with Jesus the honour of being the most picturesque college in Cambridge, and both are none the less picturesque because they hide themselves away in a corner. Dates are here a little difficult to determine, for the gate-tower and the two brick courts from King's Lane to the river are strongly marked with the stamp of medieval religion, and part of the side towards Silver Street has an air of undiluted antiquity which, in Cambridge, it is refreshing to recognise. Still, supposing the present buildings to have been begun about 1475, the gate-tower cannot have been finished long before 1500. This is clear if we compare it with the towers at Jesus, Christ's and St John's, all of which were built between 1497 and 1520, Jesus being the earliest of all. This is not the most conspicuous of them, but it is the boldest, and the arrangement of its corner turrets is especially admirable. The court on which it opens is small and simple, and its features are very much the same as those which appear in the oldest parts of St John's. The Hall on the west side is a restoration of the old Hall, which was brought into agreement with last century taste. It has a pleasant interior, and the woodwork of the doors is good. On the north side of the court is the curious sun-dial constructed by Sir Isaac Newton; the turret on which it is displayed is modern, but is an excellent ornament to the court. Beneath it is a passage to the more modern part of the college, east of which is the old chapel, a Perpendicular building much modernised by Essex in 1773.

Through the hall screens is the second court, surrounded by low, tunnel-like cloisters with plain, wide openings in each bay. This charming court owes a great deal of its beauty to the President's Lodge, which occupies the whole of the northern side. This quaint Elizabethan building, with its high gables and bulging sides, appears to advantage from every point, and the oriels of its picture-gallery, so arranged that, none being opposite another, the light is equally distributed throughout, go to make an exquisite picture which can hardly be excelled. On the opposite side of the court, however, is the small enclosure which, although known as Erasmus Court, has very little to remind us of Erasmus. Essex, who did so much harm in Cambridge, rebuilt this corner of the college in his formal manner about 1773. From the wooden bridge at the end of the court, the damage done by this addition to the river façade can be properly estimated. The bridge itself dates from 1746, and is said to have been designed by Newton on a geometrical principle. It leads to the small garden known as Erasmus' Walk.

Queens' College

The Bridge Queens' College

Returning to the eastern side of the college, we find, north of the first court, a wing in line with the gateway-tower, continuing the front of the college along King's Lane. This, which was built about 1617, is not very remarkable, and appears to have been intended for use rather than ornament. Everything north of this is modern. The northernmost range of chambers was built by Mr W. M. Fawcett in 1886. Although it is very good in its way, its juxtaposition to the new court of King's is fatal to its beauty. Here, too, Mr Bodley has been at work. His new chapel, the most recent addition to the buildings, is a pretty but not a very successful piece of work. The interior is elaborately fitted with a very complete set of stalls, and the organ-case and reredos are very fair reproductions of medieval painting. Mr Kempe's windows and the Flemish altar-piece deserve admiration, but the south side of the building has been spoiled by some very poor glass by Hardman, taken from the old chapel. Queens', on the whole, if we except the President's Lodge, depends on its delightful general effect rather than on any very special architectural merit.

In 1446 Andrew Doket, rector of St Botolph's Church, founded the College of St Bernard for a president and four fellows. The site which he chose for his foundation was east of the present college, and comprehended an oblong strip of ground running from what was then Milne Street eastwards to Trumpington Street—in fact, part of the site occupied by St Catharine's. Doket, who may be regarded as a second Edmund Gonville, was first president of his college. However, his original idea was small and its success was scarcely inevitable. Henry VI. had just founded his splendid college at the other end of Milne Street, and Doket conceived the happy idea of inducing his queen to perpetuate her name in the same way. Margaret of Anjou, who was then, as Mr Atkinson points out, only fifteen years old, showed great readiness in emulating her husband. She consented in 1448 to refound the college under the name of the Queen's College of St Margaret and St Bernard, and petitioned Henry for a charter, which was readily granted. The buildings were begun about this time on the present site. The history of Queens' College thus offers an interesting parallel to that of the similarly named college at Oxford. In both cases the first idea is due to a clerk in holy orders, who invites the reigning queen to occupy his foundation. Margaret of Anjou has been since looked upon as the chief foundress and benefactress of the college. In gratitude, the society adopted her coat-of-arms, and, although this was superseded no less than three times by other devices, it was adopted again in 1575, and is now, with the addition of a bordure, the escutcheon of the college. This magnificent piece of heraldry, which attracts all eyes by its prominent situation in the first court, recalls the claims of the House of Anjou to European sovereignty. The unfortunate history of Margaret's father, René of Provence, and her brother, the Duke of Calabria, is the key to the shield. Its quarterings include the arms of the kingdoms of Hungary, the two Sicilies and Jerusalem in the upper half, and, in the lower, those of the county of Anjou and the Duchies of Bar and Lorraine.

The thirty-six years of Doket's presidency were interrupted by the Wars of the Roses, which prevented the building from going on. Doket, however, like so many heads of houses in subsequent years, had an affection for his college which hindered him from displaying any political prejudice. In 1465, when Edward IV. was firmly established on the English throne, he applied for help to Queen Elizabeth Wydvil. This lady owed her position at court to a situation in Queen Margaret's retinue, and she readily accepted his offer. Just as her husband helped on the building of the chapel of King's, she extended her aid to this other Lancastrian foundation, and, under her protection, the work of building proceeded. The only alterations due to Yorkist patronage were a new coat-of-arms for the college, and the change of the title from Queen's College in the singular to Queens' College in the plural. The invocation of St Margaret and St Bernard was retained without alteration. The floriated cross of St Margaret and St Bernard's crosier are to be seen upon the groined roof of the gateway, and, later on, when Richard III. gave a new coat-of-arms to the college in place of that granted by Edward IV., these emblems appear surmounted by the well-known boar's head.

Doket died in 1484, and was succeeded by Thomas Wilkinson, whose rule lasted till 1505. Then followed the three years during which John Fisher, the celebrated Bishop of Rochester, was president. This great man was one of that band of scholars and divines who reformed the state of learning in England. Queens' College probably owes to him the chief episode in its history, the residence of Erasmus* within its walls. It is improbable that Erasmus was at Queens' during Fisher's presidency, as has been so generally supposed. He was invited to England by Henry VIII. soon after 1509, and Fisher had given up the presidency in 1508. No doubt, Fisher advised Erasmus, who, as Fuller says, "might have *pickt* and *chose* what house he pleased," to the cloistral seclusion of Queens'; and this is more likely than the somewhat far-fetched alternative that he was "allured with the situation of this Colledge so near the River, as Rotterdam his native place to the Sea." In fact, Erasmus was simply allured to Cambridge by the prospect of work, and does not seem to have enjoyed life there at all. Three of his letters are dated from Queens' by name, and they, as well as the rest written from no particular address in Cambridge, prove that he regarded his work there as a *pis aller*. He complained of his situation, his food and drink. Cambridge beer encouraged the most painful ailments. He wrote to a friend for a cask of Greek wine. This rare beverage was finished all too soon; when it was done, he kept the empty cask by him, that he might at least refresh himself with the smell. He was ill most of his time; he was also continually in want of money. His professorships were merely lectureships, and his pay was probably small. Had it not been for the patronage of Archbishop Warham and other lovers of learning, he might have fallen into serious straits. At no time did he realise the value of money. Doubtless, he represented himself as more unpleasantly situated than he actually was. Like most delicate men, he was very self-conscious, and expected an inordinate amount of praise and flattery, which it is hardly probable that he obtained at Cambridge. On a previous visit to Oxford, he had been the centre of a group of scholars; at Cambridge, he was isolated from his old friends. We can therefore hardly trust to his vivacious narrative for an accurate account of his Cambridge life. But, everything taken into consideration, he was seriously discontented, and was glad to leave in 1514. His memory has been more than ordinarily cherished in an University which perhaps caressed him very little in his lifetime, and his prestige has had a salutary influence on Cambridge scholarship. When he came to Cambridge, he found the old scholastic learning, which he detested, still in vogue; when he left, it was with the consciousness that he had inaugurated a new era.

The next point in the history of Queens' is its acquisition under Dr William Mey of the Carmelite house which lay between the college and the present site of King's. This house was surrendered to the society in 1538, just before the dissolution; but the interference of the Crown delayed the completion of this transaction till 1544. The ground which thus came into the possession of the president and fellows was the foundation of all their future building. Dr Mey was deprived at the accession of Queen Mary, but was restored in 1559. He lived for only a year afterwards. His next successor but one was Dr William Chaderton, of whom Fuller has preserved some curious anecdotes. He is reported to have said one day in a wedding sermon "That the choice of a wife is full of hazard, not unlike as if one in a barrel full of serpents should grope for one fish; if (saith he) he 'scape harm of the snakes, and light on a fish, he may be thought fortunate, for perhaps it may be but an eel." The ingenuity of the comparison is very characteristic of our Elizabethan universities, and is not a little in the manner of Fuller himself. Fuller, indeed, received most of what he would have called his "breeding" at Queens', and, here and at Sidney, he picked up that curiously miscellaneous knowledge which has made him one of our most entertaining prose writers. He was essentially a Cambridge man, and in all his books, however distant they are from the purpose, we trace a certain appeal to his university. He was not less positive as to its antiquity than Dr Caius, although he went less far back for its origin. His *Church History* records the foundation of Cambridge as an University by Sigebert, King of the East Anglians, and in the sequel punctiliously refers to the foundation of every college as an important event in the history of the Church. He did for Cambridge, in a more limited area, what Anthony Wood did for Oxford. His politics were of an undecided kind, and he fell into disfavour with both Parliamentarians and Royalists, but he was, in fact, a moderate partisan of the King. There is a story that he was to have been made a bishop at the Restoration, but he died before the offer was made.

John Davenant,* president from 1614 to 1622, was, as Bishop of Salisbury, one of that galaxy of prelates which relieves the darkness of the Civil Wars. He was the friend of George Herbert, whose parsonage of Bemerton was within three miles of Salisbury. He died in 1641, before affairs had come to their final climax. It is probable that he was guilty of some of those numerous idolatries which Dowsing the iconoclast destroyed on his visit to Cambridge. Dowsing visited the college on St Stephen's Day, 1643, when he "beat down 110 superstitious pictures besides Cherubim and Ingravings," and "digged up the steps for three hours." What Dowsing would say to the internal fittings of the new chapel we have no idea! After the storm had passed over and the Restoration had given back quiet to the college, its history languished: and, although it has done well in the schools, it cannot be said to have produced many men of great distinction. In Isaac Milner (* Harlow), Dean of Carlisle and President from 1788 to 1820, it had a Church historian of some reputation. Simon Patrick,* Bishop of Ely during the reigns of William III. and

Queen Anne, was a fellow here, and was one of the latest survivors of the Laudian school. His account of the opening of Edward the Confessor's tomb is preserved in the University Library in its original manuscript. He was a great theologian and something of a controversialist. Quite recently the familiar figure of Dr Campion,* Vicar of St Botolph's and Honorary Canon of Ely, and President of Queens' for the last five years of his life, has been removed from Cambridge. His successor is Dr Herbert Ryle of King's, who holds with the office the Hulsean Professorship of Divinity.

CHAPTER XI

ST CATHARINE'S COLLEGE

It has been said that the decorous quadrangle of St Catharine's gives the stranger the impression of an old manor house rather than of a college; and the trees which guard it on the side of Trumpington Street are certainly a party to the illusion. The western front of the college, which occupies one side of King's Lane, has a more definitely scholastic air. For the most part the buildings are uninteresting. The tiny court at the north-west angle dates from 1626; the rest of the college is the fruit of a rebuilding which went on slowly from 1680 to 1755. Loggan, who published his illustrations soon after the work was begun, figures, with some optimism, an eastern façade with a central cupola. This, however, was never attempted. The chapel is an interesting piece of Queen Anne architecture, dating from 1704; and lately a fine organ by Norman & Beard of Norwich has been placed in it. In the present century, the Hall has been restored in the Gothic style, but otherwise no radical alteration has been made.

St Catharine's is, in a certain sense, the daughter of King's, for its founder was Robert Woodlark,* provost of the latter college. The reason for its foundation is not very obvious: it was probably merely a pious act on the part of Woodlark, of whom we know very little beyond this. The site on which it stood occupied the greater part of that oblong space which still is bounded on the north by King's Lane and on the south by Silver (then Small Bridges) Street. Even now the space is somewhat cramped by houses; then the college was thoroughly "town-bound," as Fuller puts it. However, although one of the smallest colleges in Cambridge, it has given, in comparison with its size, more famous men to England than any college in either University. These men are all clergy, and their names are among the most reverend in Church history. Seventy-four years after the foundation of the college, Edwin Sandys* became master. He is chiefly known as Archbishop of York and as a translator of the Bible, and, while in exile abroad during Mary's reign, he cultivated friendly relations with foreign Protestant churches. As Master of St Catharine's and Vice-Chancellor, he went through a critical experience, which is narrated by Fuller. The Duke of Northumberland, who was at Cambridge in the hope of intercepting Mary's progress from the Eastern Counties to London, ordered Sandys to preach before him at the University Church. Sandys was a timid man and had very little faith in Lady Jane Grey's cause, so that the order caused him some perplexity. He rose at a very early hour next morning, and took the *sortes Biblicae* after the approved manner of the sixteenth century. The text at which his Bible opened was the sixteenth and seventeenth verses of the first chapter of Joshua, "All that thou commandest us we will do, and whithersoever thou sendest us we will go. According as we hearkened unto Moses in all things, so will we hearken unto thee: only the Lord thy God be with thee, as he was with Moses." He preached from this text in so politic a manner that no one could find a handle of accusation against him. The exacting Northumberland came back to Cambridge after a short tour in Suffolk, well aware that his enterprise was over, and with the forlorn hope that, if he proclaimed Mary queen, he might win his pardon. He invited Sandys to join in the proclamation with him, but the Vice-Chancellor refused with an answer that must have been a very cold comfort to Northumberland. The Duke, however, went through the business mechanically at the old Market Cross, and was arrested very soon afterwards at his lodgings in King's. Sandys escaped to the Netherlands, and returned when Elizabeth came to the throne. He is buried at Southwell, where the archbishops of York had one of their palaces.

John Overall, Bishop of Lichfield, and afterwards of Norwich, another of the translators of the Bible, was master from 1598 to 1607. The college leaned throughout its history to the Puritanic side of the religious question, and Richard Sibbes, master from 1626 to 1635, is one of those strongly Puritan divines who had the advantage of an University education. His evangelical theology, rich in quaint phrase and full of ingenious learning, is still popular with serious readers, although his fame has been somewhat overshadowed by the greater names of Bunyan, Baxter, and John Owen. In spite of this spiritual activity, it appears that the college was about this time in a very bad and ruinous state, and, on the side of Trumpington Street, was excessively cramped for room. During the mastership of John Hills, Sibbes' predecessor, John Gostlin, the eccentric master of Caius, gave the Bull Inn, which was his personal property, to the college, and thus the society was enabled to enlarge its frontiers. Nevertheless, the commotions of the Civil Wars delayed operations until long after the Restoration, when Dr John Eachard, master in 1675, carried out the longed-for improvements. There is no college whose external appearance belies a medieval foundation more than St Catharine's.

Side by side with Sibbes we may reckon the famous Dissenting preacher, Edmund Calamy, who was also a member of this college and was connected with Sidney as well. But, after the Restoration and Eachard's improvements, St Catharine's settled down again to its episcopal traditions. Sir William Dawes, Eachard's successor from 1697 to 1714, was a worthy but in no way remarkable Archbishop of York. During his time, however, the society received a famous member in the militant Benjamin Hoadly,* Bishop first of Bangor, then of Hereford, then of Salisbury, and lastly of Winchester. It is curious that Hoadly, the typical Latitudinarian, as the ugly phrase goes, of his age, and his opponent, the no less typical High Churchman, William Law, were members of the two Cambridge colleges which had shown most activity on the Puritan side, St Catharine's and Emmanuel. Hoadly's book, *On the Nature of the Kingdom and Church of Christ*, is his chief claim to celebrity, as the doctrines which it advocated gave rise to the Bangorian Controversy and were the cause of many polemical treatises which have a distinct literary rank.

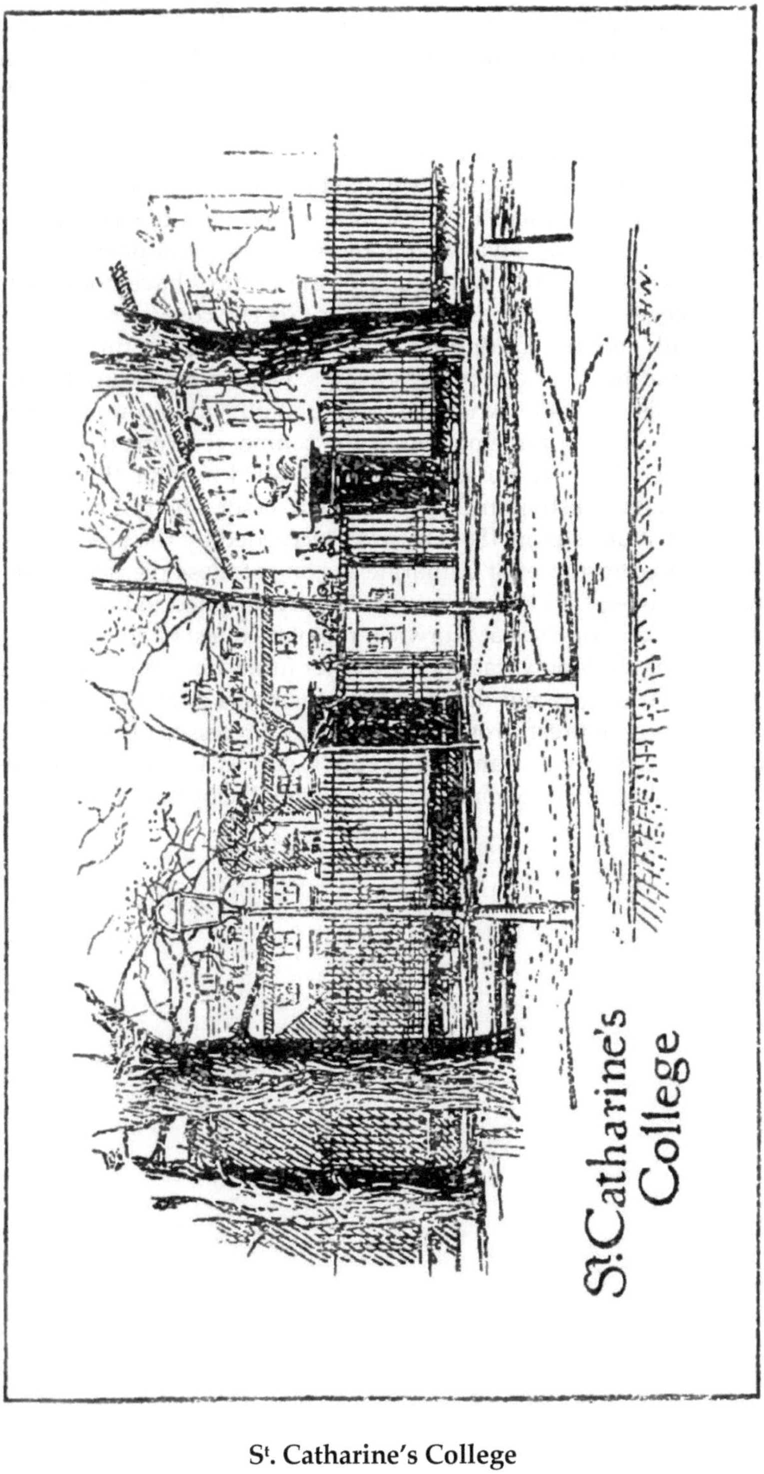

S[t]. Catharine's College

Other members of St Catharine's about the end of the seventeenth century were Dr John Lightfoot,* master from 1650 to 1675, illustrious as an Orientalist; John Strype, the ecclesiastical antiquarian, who died in 1737 at the advanced age of ninety-four; and John Ray,* the naturalist, who died in 1705. In 1704, during Dawes' mastership, the chapel was consecrated by Bishop Simon Patrick of Ely, who was a member of Queens' College. In 1714, Dawes was succeeded by Thomas Sherlock,* whose oratorical powers gained him the Bishoprick of London. His sermons, which are specimens of a cold and stilted kind of eloquence, are read no longer, but his name survives as that of one of the great preachers of the last century. His successors down to the end of the century have not much interest outside the college. The long mastership of Dr Procter* covers almost the first half of the nineteenth century. During his time, the versatile Dr Turton* was fellow of the college and held various professorships. He became Dean of Westminster and eventually Bishop of Ely, where he continued till within comparatively recent years. He is perhaps best remembered as the composer of one of the most beautiful hymn-tunes which we possess—the tune called by him "Ely." The college produced yet another bishop in Dr Procter's successor, Henry Philpott, who was made Bishop of Worcester in 1861. He was succeeded by the present master, Dr Robinson. The mastership of St Catharine's is one of those pleasant posts, which, like Pembroke College at Oxford, have a canonry attached to them. The canonry belonging to St Catharine's is at Norwich, the pleasantest of all English cathedral cities, and, during the long vacation, the master fulfils his term of residence in the Norwich close. Among recent distinguished members of St Catharine's we may mention Dr George Forrest Browne, late Disney Professor of Archæology, who succeeded Dean Gregory as Canon of St Paul's, and was, in 1897, translated from the suffragan Bishoprick of Stepney to the revived Bishoprick of Bristol.

CHAPTER XII

JESUS COLLEGE

Bishop Alcock's gate-tower, a few years earlier than those of Christ's and St John's, and almost contemporary with that of Queens', forms a charming prelude to this beautiful college. Its stepped battlements are original, and its plan is more domestic than those of the other towers, which have a very monastic appearance. The founder's coat-of-arms, the three cocks which the college has ever since borne as its cognisance, appear on various parts of the tower and in the roof of the gateway; but the statue of Bishop Alcock and a good deal of the decoration are new.[5] The tower is the entrance to the outer court of the college, whose ivy-grown buildings date from 1641. They are very fair late Gothic work and carefully follow Alcock's tower in their general lines; they are due to Richard Sterne (master, 1633-1644 and again in 1660), but they were not actually finished until the beginning of George the First's reign. They occupy three sides of the court; the western side is open, affording a good view of the towers in the centre of the town. From the opposite side a low postern gateway (part of the original work) leads into the inner court of the college, round which the public buildings are situated. The Hall is on the north side; opposite it is the Master's Lodge and the nave of the chapel. The Library occupies the west side, and the northern transept of the chapel the east side. This was originally the cloister of the nunnery which was superseded by the college. The cloisters which exist are subsequent to the founding of the college, and for some time were shut in, like those at Wilton House. In the last century, however, they were opened to the court, and now they are simply of the ordinary covered type, without any wall of partition. A few years ago, while repairs were being carried on in the eastern wall of these cloisters, just north of the transept-end of the chapel, a beautiful triple arch of the Early English period was laid open, and may now be examined. This was probably the entrance to the nuns' chapter-house. It is a very unique and delicate piece of work, dating probably from about 1240, and compares very well with the excellent work of that period to be found in Cambridgeshire.

[5] The tower may be compared with the palace which Alcock built at Ely. Both are admirable examples of their style.

Jesus College

Part of the chapel dates from the foundation of the nunnery, but a great deal of it is Early English, and the whole building was remodelled by Alcock on the collegiate principle. He seems to have cut away the aisles of the convent church, leaving only the north choir aisle; he left the transepts unchanged, save for a set of Perpendicular windows with scanty tracery, which are repeated in the nave and choir. His east window has been taken away and the Early English triplet restored. He thus made an ordinary monastic building into an aisleless cruciform church, differing from a college chapel only in that it retains a nave, in which respect it is unique. He also added the Perpendicular upper storey to the central tower, the lower half of which is Early English, and corresponds in its interior arcading with the arches in the cloister. The upper storey of this earlier tower had fallen in 1297. On the whole, one can hardly give unqualified praise to Alcock for his treatment of the building, but he made it answer his purposes very well. Moreover, he gave it some beautiful stalls and a screen. Unfortunately, these ornaments offended Georgian taste. The restoration of the chapel in the last century was a wonderful proceeding. The walls were daubed with yellow relieved by a low black dado, the ceiling was plastered, the best part of the woodwork was removed to Landbeach Church, five miles on the way to Ely, and the central lantern was closed up, so that the fine arcade was completely hidden. To-day, however, we are able to see the chapel without these encumbrances, for the restoration, begun in 1845 and continued to our own day, has made it the most historical interior in Cambridge. The south transept with its eastern gallery is for the most part Norman of a very simple order, coeval with the foundation of the monastery. The central tower, the choir and chancel are Early English, save for Alcock's additions on the south side, and the remaining aisle, which contains Decorated work. The arcaded lancets on the north side of the chancel should be noticed: this singularly graceful arrangement is almost unique. There is, however, an example, completer and perhaps finer, at Cherry Hinton, within an hour's walk of Cambridge. Another specimen of local work is the double piscina, whose splendid mouldings, crossing each other in the head of the arch, and reminding one of well-folded linen, are only to be found in three or four churches in, or immediately round the town. I have spoken of Alcock's Perpendicular work, which is of a kind more domestic than ecclesiastical. The stalls and screen are rather more than forty years old, but they show a taste of a kind unusual at that time, and are much improved by the dim light of the whole building. This dimness is due to the stained glass, which is all modern. The glass in the lancets is by Hardman; it is not very good, but it is unobtrusive. That in Alcock's two choir windows was put in rather earlier by the restorers of 1845-9; it is the great defect in their work. But the eleven perpendicular windows of the antechapel, including the enormous south window, have been filled with glass by Sir Edward Burne-Jones and Mr William Morris; and their magnificent, if somewhat secular, work, serves to hide the shallowness and unoriginality of the stonework. It is a pity that, in one or two places, the colours already show signs of decaying; but, on the whole, the two great artists seldom collaborated to such purpose or found such excellent material for their work. The organ at the west end is new, and there is perhaps too little space for it. The older organ, a small instrument with a triptych front, is in the choir aisle, and has an appearance strongly suggestive of the bygone monasticism of the place.

The rest of the Court, Hall, Library and Master's Lodge are much as the founder left them, although their outer shell has been from time to time considerably altered. The Hall, with its dark lobby on the ground floor and its staircase, is a fine room, occupying the position of the convent refectory. There are some good portraits here and in the Combination Room, including one of Cranmer in the manner of Holbein. The Hall was wainscoted early in the last century. Since then and since the completion of the outer court, the college has received no structural additions to its main body.[6] Within the last thirty years, however, the need for accommodation has increased; and we owe to it, first, Messrs Carpenter and Ingelow's brick range of buildings north of the college and their houses for married tutors; and, secondly, the great building, also of brick, which Waterhouse built about 1869 at the end of the garden east of the chapel. His work here is better than usual, and forms a picturesque outpost to the colleges as one crosses the end of Midsummer Common by the Newmarket Road. The Jesus close, with its great palisade of trees and its view of the boathouses on one side and the venerable chapel tower on the other, almost rivals the Backs in beauty.

John Alcock, Bishop of Ely, whose chantry chapel by Torregiano is one of the chief glories of his diocesan cathedral, left a more important monument to posterity in the shape of Jesus College. In 1497 he obtained a charter for his foundation, which succeeded a house of Benedictine nuns, existing under the invocation of the Blessed Virgin and St Rhadegund. This religious establishment had been founded in 1133 by favour of Malcolm IV. of Scotland, Earl of Huntingdon, and its chief benefactress was Constance of France, daughter of Louis VI. and widow of King Stephen's son Eustace. Started under these auspices, it became one of the most important conventual houses in Cambridge, and received in its various vicissitudes help from divers quarters. In 1297, the chapel tower fell; there were fires in 1343 and 1376; in 1390, the buildings were seriously injured by a storm. It is possible that the morality of the house, which enjoyed great popularity, grew lax, and that the change was necessary. This was at all events the excuse for the disestablishment of the convent. However, Mr Clark, in his chapter on the college, proves with great likelihood that these complaints were merely superficial. The fact is that the demand for education was increasing, and the supply was furnished at the expense of the old monastic houses. At its dissolution the revenue of the nunnery was considerable. Alcock kept up the traditions of the site by dedicating his college to the Blessed Virgin, St John the evangelist and St Rhadegund, but the title was soon exchanged for the name of Jesus. By its foundation a precedent was set for other colleges to follow. After Jesus, other foundations were erected on the site of some monastery or hospital; even some of those existing, such as Queens', bought up monastic property and enriched themselves with it.

Jesus College took for its first shield the curious device of the five wounds of Christ. But in 1575, it received its present coat-of-arms in memory of its founder.

[6] With the exception of the range of buildings (1822) forming an extension of the east side of Cloister Court.

The three cocks' heads erased have always been a feature of the college very much in evidence; they appear constantly in the buildings, and, in the cloister court, may still be seen the two cocks, one of whom says to the other from the library wall "ἐγὼ εἰμὶ ἀλεκτὼϱ" (I am a cock), while the other, from the hall, bears in his mouth a similar scroll inscribed "οὗτως καί ἐγὼ" (And so am I). Soon after Alcock's time, the college brought forth a fruit of the new learning in the shape of Thomas Cranmer,* who was a fellow here for some time. He lost his fellowship by his marriage. He contracted an alliance with the niece of the landlady of the Dolphin, an inn close to what is now All Saints' Passage, and, having resigned his fellowship in consequence, lived at the inn for some time. Cambridge was a great university for reformers, and at this time a number of men who afterwards became distinguished for the novelty of their opinions were in residence. The college has honoured Cranmer's memory, and one of its most popular social clubs is named after him. Readers of history know that Cranmer was no less eminent as statesman and man of letters than as reformer, and his college may be justly proud of him. His portraits are interesting. The picture in the Hall is supposed to be a copy by Reynolds from an older picture. In the Combination Room is the portrait dated 1548, similar to the portrait of 1546 by Fliccius, now in the National Portrait Gallery. And in the Master's Lodge is another portrait which is probably a copy of the last. Both these latter portraits have been attributed to Holbein.

The name of William Bancroft,* Archbishop of Canterbury, brings us to the reign of James I. That wise monarch, on his visit to the University, professed a wish the justice of which most of us have acknowledged, that, were he at Cambridge, he would "pray at King's, dine at Trinity and sleep at Jesus." The master at this date was Dr John Duport. Jesus was, of all colleges, most loyal to the Stewarts. Dr William Beale, master in 1632, and removed to St John's in the next year, was a constant royalist. His successor, Dr Richard Sterne,* was entirely of the same opinion. He, with Dr Beale and Dr Martin of Queens', formed a sort of syndicate for melting college plate and sending it to the King; and was accordingly arrested by Cromwell and imprisoned in the Tower. His friends shared the same fate; but Sterne was probably especially marked out for this favour, as he had been Laud's chaplain and had attended him on the scaffold. After the Restoration, he resumed his mastership, but he was removed in the same year to higher honours. In 1664 he was made Archbishop of York, and died in 1683. His portrait in the Hall was presented by his nephew Laurence Sterne (* Alan Ramsay) who was later on a pensioner of Jesus. Laurence Sterne, who also took holy orders, was a different type of man from his uncle. The great sentimentalist is one of the most distinguished *alumni* of Jesus, although he did very little at college. As author of *Tristram Shandy* and *The Sentimental Journey*, as fashionable preacher and as wit, the eccentric Vicar of Coxwold has achieved a reputation only a little below that of Fielding, on the one hand, and of Swift, on the other.

In the meantime, Dr Sterne was succeeded by Dr John Pearson, who, after shedding his lustre on several colleges, became Master of Trinity and finally Bishop of Chester. It is fortunate for his various colleges that the honours of this great theologian have been so divided. About this time we come to the revered name of

Tobias Rustat (* Lely) Gentleman of the Robes, who was a great benefactor to the college and founded the Rustat scholarships. Even to-day the Rustat scholars of Jesus wear a peculiar gown of their own, differing slightly from the gowns of the rest of the college. Rustat is buried in the chapel, like Dr Ashton at St John's, and the college has reason to remember his name with the gratitude which Ashton's liberality excited in Thomas Baker. He may, indeed, be regarded almost as a second founder of the college.

The masters of the eighteenth century were, for the most part, stately and important men who received a great deal of promotion. Dr Charles Ashton, of whom the college possesses two portraits, was master for fifty-one years, from 1701 to 1752. In his time there was at Jesus a whilom famous scholar, Dr John Jortin,* to whom we owe the very careful but extremely dull life of Erasmus. He was a popular divine, and combined the lucrative posts of Archdeacon of London, Rector of St Dunstan's in the East, and Vicar of Kensington. Dr Ashton was succeeded by Dr Philip Yonge, who was master for six years, and was then made Bishop of Bristol, being eventually translated to Norwich in 1761. His portrait in the Master's Lodge is said to be by Reynolds. His successor, Dr Lynford Caryl (* from a portrait by Wright of Derby), is remarkable for little save his picturesque name. He, in his turn, give place to Richard Beadon,* who was removed to Gloucester in 1789 and died as Bishop of Bath and Wells in 1824.

When Dr William Pearce (* Beechey) was Master—he was also Master of the Temple and Dean of Ely—Samuel Taylor Coleridge (* from Washington Allston) came into residence. Coleridge was two years younger than Wordsworth, and came up after the elder poet had gone abroad to watch the French Revolution. Less fortunate than Wordsworth, he left Cambridge in 1794 without his degree, in this anticipating Tennyson. Like most poets, he formed few friendships while at Cambridge, and took no considerable part in the academic life of his day. Milton, whose genius was eminently academic, is the exception to this rule. We find it difficult, on the other hand, to look upon Coleridge as an University man, and the same difficulty would occur with regard to Wordsworth, were it not for his minute account of his life at St John's. Shelley, also, who was twenty years younger than Coleridge, took no degree at Oxford. Nevertheless, the colleges of these unsatisfactory students have, since their death, conspired to honour them, and doubtless to many Jesus men Coleridge is their *genius loci* very much as Shelley is to men at University College.

Dr Clarke, Professor of Mineralogy (* Opie) was a contemporary of Coleridge who preferred to close his University life in the orthodox way. He died in 1822, when Dr French* had succeeded Dr Pearce in the mastership. The days of ecclesiastical preferment ceased with Dr Pearce, and his successors were content to hold quiet country livings with their mastership. This was the case with the late master, Dr Corrie,* who divided his time between the college and his pleasant rectory of Newton-in-the-Isle. The last ten years of his rule were remarkable for the supremacy of Jesus as head of the river, when the college was full of oarsmen like Mr Shafto and the late Mr Edward Prest. It is matter of history how, when the boat "went down" for the first time in ten years, the Jesus men appeared on the river and the towing-path in mourning. In 1885 Dr Morgan (* Collier), the brother of a celebrated Oxford man, the late Sir George Osborne Morgan, became master, and under him the college, if less successful on the river, has preserved its old reputation. Among the modern sons of the college we should remember Dr Wilkinson,* the present Anglican Bishop in North and Central Europe, originally Missionary Bishop in Zululand, and the Rev. Osmond Fisher,* Honorary Fellow, to whose antiquarian zeal the college is indebted for the excavation of its monastic remains.

CHAPTER XIII

CHRIST'S COLLEGE

Christ's may be cited as a fair specimen of the normal Cambridge college. Its court and gate-tower have suffered considerably since they were first built, having been recased with stone in 1724. This pious work was undertaken with funds supplied by Dr Thomas Lynford, fellow of the college and Archdeacon of Barnstaple, and is as well done as one can expect of anything so radical. Two years later, the west front of Pembroke was treated in the same way, and the two may be cited together as in some measure a vindication of the early Georgian restorer. All that was done was to make the face of the college flat and remove all superficial irregularities, while the general lines of the building were scrupulously maintained. Dr Lynford is not responsible for the interior of the court, which belongs to a later part of the century, and is due to Essex or one of his kind. Originally, we may imagine a quadrangle of dark red brick, very like the courts at St John's and Queens'. The gate-towers of all three colleges are very similar; in that of Christ's the foundress' statue is a modern addition. The present chapel, north of the court, is substantially the chapel of Lady Margaret Beaufort's foundation, and the small vestries are partly of that date. As for the rest, it is very good work of the middle of the last century imposed on Italian Gothic, and the antechapel, with its wooden columns, is admirable. Above the altar is a good window by some German or Flemish artist, not unlike the east window at Peterhouse, and of much the same period. The organ, in a gallery north of the sanctuary, is by Father Smith, and the case is an excellent piece of woodwork. At the west end is a curious portrait of the foundress, and the chapel has a strong historical interest as the burying-place of the Cambridge Platonists, Cudworth, More, and Mede.

Between the Chapel and Hall stands the Master's Lodge, placed so as to communicate with both. The Hall has been very well restored, and is now a good Gothic hall, with an oriel full of excellent portrait glass, representing all the worthies of the college, from the Lady Margaret down to Paley in his archdeacon's apron and Darwin in his doctor's gown. Beyond the hall, and facing westwards, is the lovely building of 1642, which is usually attributed to Inigo Jones. A range of older buildings, constituting the south side of the court, used to impede the full view of this beautiful structure; but these were moved back early in the century, and rebuilt in the hideous taste of the time. However, we are the gainers by it. Although the work at Clare is, as a whole, a better specimen of the period, the Christ's building has the advantage of perfect uniformity, and is an excellent example of the transition from Renaissance Gothic to the style of which Wren is the chief exponent.

Its base is pierced by a gateway leading into the famous garden, a classic resort which is a very competent rival of any garden at Oxford. Of the new buildings at the north-eastern extremity of the college, it is unnecessary to say anything; they are moderate, but are hardly worth a detailed inspection. Their architect was Mr J. J. Stevenson. Within the last three years Messrs Bodley and Garner have been employed upon the street front, and, needless to say, have restored it with their usual conservative skill.

Christ's College

For the beginnings of Christ's College we must go back to the year 1436. William Bingham, Rector of St John Zachary in the city of London, founded a small hostel or Grammar College in connection with Clare, and placed it on a site which is now occupied by the western part of King's College Chapel and a portion of the great court of King's. Four years later, Henry VI.'s great experiment forced Bingham to seek other quarters, which he eventually found in Preachers' Street, the thoroughfare leading from the Barnwell Gate to the Dominican Friary. Here he re-founded his college under the picturesque name of God's House, which it had already borne in its former position. But, like so many similar institutions, its revenues languished. Bingham's society was to consist of a master with the title of Proctor, and of twenty-four scholars. By the beginning of the sixteenth century, the house maintained only four scholars besides the Proctor. There is a story that the great John Fisher, Bishop of Rochester, was bred at this hostel; and that his affection for it was the cause which moved him to bring its destitution to the notice of his friend, Lady Margaret Beaufort. It is, at all events, more than certain that Fisher, who guided his patroness in her pious resolves, called her attention to the case, and so laid the foundation, as it were, of Christ's and St John's. There is no satisfactory evidence as to the time at which she conceived the idea of founding St John's. Probably, the notion of a college had taken her fancy long before, and it is not unlikely that the opportunity of founding two colleges presented itself at one time. At any rate, her first work was to re-establish God's House in 1505. The task of converting St John's Hospital into St John's College required several years of preliminaries and formalities. But in God's House she had a college already to her hand. Henry VI. had apparently promised Bingham some compensation for the removal of the house, but the greater work of founding King's and the civil troubles which soon engrossed the crown had prevented him from fulfilling his promise. The Lady Margaret, devoted to the memory of the "royal saint," endowed the society on the scale approved by him, and provided funds for the maintenance of a master, twelve fellows and forty-seven scholars. And "from her singular devotion to the name of Jesus Christ"—the same motive which had prompted Alcock to call his foundation Jesus College—she founded the college under the invocation of Christ. We have thus two colleges at Cambridge which recall the popular devotion of the Name of Jesus, then lately established and approved.

It may or may not be true that the foundress had rooms reserved for her use in the Master's Lodge. The story seems contrary to the spirit of that age or of any other, but a point may have been stretched in her favour. The testimony for this legend rests upon an anecdote told by Fuller. "The Lady Margaret," he says, "once ... came to Christ's College to behold it when partly built, and looking out of a window, saw the dean call a faulty scholar to correction, to whom she said 'lente, lente,' gently, gently, as accounting it better to mitigate his punishment than to procure his pardon; mercy and justice making the best medley to offenders." This is scarcely sufficient authority for the tradition. There are no less than four portraits of the Lady Margaret in the college, the best of which is perhaps that at the west end of the chapel, closely resembling the picture in the hall at St John's. The Combination Room also contains a portrait of Bishop Fisher, and both these pious friends of learning are commemorated in the oriel of the Hall. From the foundation of the college onwards, its history has been peaceful and comparatively uneventful. In its early years, it seems to have anticipated the lodging-house system, for we are told that some of the scholars were lodged in the Brazen George, an inn opposite the college, and that the doors of this hostelry were closed and opened at the same time as the doors of the college.

Leland the antiquary and Hugh Latimer were among the earlier members of the college. But the history of Christ's is centred in one event, the seven years' residence of John Milton, who entered as a pensioner in 1625, and went down with his Master's degree in 1632. "John Milton of London," the entry runs in English "son of John Milton, was initialed in the elements of letters under Mr Gill, Master of St Paul's School; was admitted a lesser pensioner Feb. 12th, 1624 [O.S.] under Mr Chappell, and paid entrance fee 10s." Mr Chappell, on the authority of Dr Johnson, is said to have flogged the poet. "There is reason to believe that Milton was regarded in his college with no great fondness. That he obtained no fellowship is certain, but the unkindness with which he was treated was not merely negative." Milton himself says enough to make the truth of this statement at least doubtful; for his language, ten years after his departure from Cambridge, is not merely the language of a man who had forgotten old grudges, but breathes a lively affection for his college. The flogging possibly took place; the University was then nothing but a large public school, and each college was a separate boarding-house. Milton, when he went up, was just sixteen, and boys of sixteen are not past flogging. If he went down without a fellowship, he was surely, in spite of that, a most promising student. His Latin verses, which we still read as we read Ovid and Propertius, are the finest poetry, and not mere academical exercises; his skill in Italian marks a degree of culture unknown even in that Italianised age. In addition to his scholarship, he possessed extraordinary personal beauty, which gives him among poets something of that eminence possessed by Raffaelle among painters. We are told that he was called the "Lady of the College." And, while at Christ's, he wrote some of his most lasting works, including the famous Hymn on the Nativity, which was written in 1629. His verses on Hobson, the University carrier, are well known, and *Lycidas*, the elegy on his college friend, Edward King, appeared at Cambridge in 1637. His noble *Verses at a Solemn Musick*, containing some of the finest and most imaginative lines in English, belong to this early period. The master under whom his residence took place was Dr Thomas Bainbrigge, master from 1620 to 1645. Cromwell had gone down from Sidney before Milton came up to Christ's, but he was still in the neighbourhood of Cambridge. Milton's mulberry-tree, the Palladium of the college, may or may not be Milton's; but to believe the tradition does no violence to our faith. The memory of Milton had a more than usually potent influence on another poet, Wordsworth.

> Among the band of my compeers was one
> Whom chance had stationed in the very room
> Honoured by Milton's name. O temperate Bard!
> Be it confest that, for the first time, seated
> Within thy innocent lodge and oratory,
> One of a festive circle, I poured out

Libations, to thy memory drank, till pride
And gratitude grew dizzy in a brain
Never excited by the fumes of wine
Before that hour, or since.

And this, from internal evidence, must have been on a winter Sunday afternoon before chapel! For the inebriated poet, always a sad idler at Cambridge, had to run back "ostrich-like" to chapel, where he arrived late and, full of wine and Milton, swaggered up to his place through "the inferior throng of plain Burghers." Here was a young gentleman who deserved flogging!

But the presence of Milton must not allow us to forget the band of contemplative scholars and philosophers who, in his time, were the ruling influence in the college, and now lie beneath the chapel floor. The course of the reformed and Puritan doctrines was largely determined by the study of Platonic philosophy, just as the Aristotelian system had allied itself to Catholic theology. Platonism in Cambridge is the result of two opposing forces: on the positive side, the teaching of Erasmus; on the negative side, the publication of Hobbes' *Leviathan* in 1651. This book received many reputations from Cambridge men; two of the best known are the work of Dr Bramhall of Sidney, Bishop of Derry and afterwards Primate of Ireland, and of Dr Cumberland of Magdalene, the painful Bishop of Peterborough. But the most effective opposition to Hobbes' materialistic and mathematical science came from Christ's. The first of the Cambridge Platonists was the meditative Mede, who died in 1638. He was a fellow of the college in Milton's time, and spent his days in wandering about the college backs and fields, absorbed in mystical speculation, of which the eventual outcome was his work on the Apocalypse. In the evening, members of the college would resort to his rooms, and he would ask them "*Quid dubitas?* What doubts have you met in your studies to-day?" and, having heard their answers, would set their minds at rest and dismiss them with prayer. But Mede was scarcely so remarkable as Henry More, the author of the *Mystery of Godliness* and other books, who devoted his life at Cambridge to Platonic speculations, and even extended his enquiries to the Neo-Platonic writers and the Hebrew Cabala. Ralph Cudworth* was three years his junior, and survived him one year. This man, the greatest of the company, was Master of Clare for some time, and, in 1654, became Master of Christ's, where he remained, unmoved by the Restoration, till his death in 1688. He was the most powerful of Hobbes' adversaries, and his *True Intellectual System of the Universe*, published in 1678, is a fairly convincing counterblast to the *Leviathan*. However, Cudworth was rather a talented pedant than a genius: he lessened the value of his work by recondite allusions, and his critical capacity was impaired by prejudice. But, in that age of laborious theology, Cudworth's book deserves a position next to, although far below, Leighton's commentary on St Peter.

It is a somewhat melancholy fact that the only other poet of whom Christ's can boast besides Milton is that master of tortured conceits, Francis Quarles. Curiously enough, the portrait, probably of Quarles, in the Combination Room, which bears the motto "Nec ingratus nec inutilis videar vixisse" was at one time supposed to be that of Milton. But the college has had eminent students in other departments.

Dr Seth Ward,* a little younger than Milton, is known as the Bishop of Salisbury during the time of James II. and the Revolution. In 1766, at the age of twenty-three, William Paley* was elected a fellow, and remained at Cambridge for ten years. Paley's early life is said to have been careless and riotous. One morning, however, when lying late in bed, a friend and boon-companion came into his room, and treated him to what is sometimes known as a "straight talk." This admonition awakened Paley's conscience, and led in time to the publication of the famous *Evidences of Christianity* and to the Archdeaconry of Carlisle. In all probability, no historical name is so often on the undergraduate's lips—not always with blessings—as the name of this reclaimed ne'er-do-weel. The *Evidences*, as is well known, form part of the subjects for the Previous Examination or Little-Go, and have in this capacity given birth to an especial department of literature in the shape of "Paley Sheets" and other *précis* of the heavy work. A less logical but more human theologian was John Kaye,* master from 1814 to 1830, and Bishop successively of Bristol and Lincoln.

If, among statesmen, Christ's can put forward Lord Liverpool, famous for his interminable ministry of more than twenty years, she has had in science, a son who is as famous in his branch of study as Milton is in poetry. This was Charles Robert Darwin (* Ouless) who came up to Christ's in the twenties with the intention of taking holy orders. At Cambridge, however, he found such opportunities for research that he abandoned his design, and, at the recommendation of Professor Henslow, who then held the botanical chair, went out as naturalist to the *Beagle*. This was the beginning of his scientific career and of the revolution in biological science which he effected. A tablet with his profile in relief has been placed in the room occupied by him, which is at present occupied by the Norrisian Professor of Divinity, Dr Armitage Robinson. To-day Christ's not only claims as its master Dr John Peile, the eminent classical philologist, but the greatest of living scholars who have devoted themselves to the study of their own language—the editor of Langland and Chaucer, Professor Skeat. And Cambridge men will always remember with pleasure that Christ's was the college of the most pleasant of all English versifiers, Charles Stuart Calverley (then Blayds) who not only, by his light verses, added to the gaiety of the nation, but, by his translation of Theocritus, increased the range of English poetry.

CHAPTER XIV

ST JOHN'S COLLEGE

The first court of St John's is almost as composite as the Great Court of Trinity, and the want of harmony between its parts is rather painfully evident. The chapel, however, is the only important extension of the original plan as carried out by the Lady Margaret's executors, and the rest of the court survives with certain changes. The gateway of the college is one of the gate-towers so characteristic of Cambridge, and is perhaps the most beautiful of all. One of the great advantages of St John's is that it is built of red brick, which, with time, has assumed a mellow appearance; and thus it is, in certain respects, one of the most picturesque colleges in the University. The court and tower belong to 1520. Above the doorway, on the street side, are the arms of Lady Margaret, supported by the Beaufort antelopes, on a ground in which the daisy, the foundress' punning emblem, occurs very lavishly. Although much obliterated by time, this is still a very good piece of heraldic sculpture. Other familiar signs, which the least archæological undergraduate learns to recognise, are the Tudor rose and Beaufort portcullis. Above this elaborate armorial display is a figure of St John the Evangelist, added in 1662. Lady Margaret's statue is to be found in an ugly niche over the entrance to the Hall screens; it is in a pseudo-classical taste, and exaggerates her pious emaciation of feature.

The Hall has been altered a good deal, but it is an interesting apartment, long, dark and narrow, like a conventual refectory. Its darkness is due partly to the fine wainscoting, which is of the linen-pattern, partly to the deep colours of the heraldic windows, whose interest is historical rather than artistic. The fresco of the upper part is not very successful. At the end of the hall is a curious portrait of the foundress, in the manner of Lucas van Heere, which bears comparison with her picture in Christ's. She is supported by full-length portraits of Archbishop Williams and Ralph Hare, benefactors to the college. One of the most interesting pictures is the well-known portrait of Wordsworth by Pickersgill; and the modern portrait of Professor Palmer in full Arab attire (John Collier) usually attracts comment. St John's Hall is not rich in portraits, a deficiency which is remedied by the collection at the Lodge.

S[t]. John's College

St. John's College

No other college unfolds its architectural history in so leisurely a way as St John's. We pass from the first to the second court, from 1520 to 1598. In the latter year, Ralph Symons, who was supplying Dr Nevile at Trinity with designs, began to build this beautiful quadrangle. Mary Cavendish, Countess of Shrewsbury, is the benefactress to whom the college is indebted, and her statue occupies the niche over the gate-tower between this and the third court. Some will have it that this is the best piece of contemporary building in Cambridge, and it certainly has a peculiar charm, due to its studious, sober air. The sole ornaments of this gabled enclosure are the two charming oriels in the centre of the north and south side, and the gate-tower, which is not unlike the similar tower at Hampton Court. Along the first floor of the north side of the court runs the long gallery, once a part of the Master's Lodge, but now the Combination Room. It is the best Combination Room in Oxford or Cambridge. At present it is divided into two parts by a wainscoting, but this hinders the general effect very little. The plastered ceiling is very richly ornamented with pendants and formal arabesques, and has much in common with other splendid ceilings of the same date. When the doors of the inner room and of the library beyond are both open, an incomparable vista is obtained, and the two apartments are transformed into a single gallery.

As a matter of fact, a landing, approached from the second court by a picturesque oak staircase, separates the Combination Room from the Library, which occupies the whole north side of the somewhat gloomy third court. Over the door are the arms of Lord Keeper Williams, impaled on the coat of his see of Lincoln. This famous prelate contributed entirely to its erection, and his initials and the date 1624 are lettered in white stone outside the western oriel. It was completed in 1628, and remains unaltered, a very charming specimen of Italian Gothic. Its interior, with its high timber roof and fine bookcases, is the *beau idéal* of a library interior. There are two stories: the upper contains the valuable collection of ancient books and the bequests of various benefactors such as Matthew Prior, the lower is devoted to more modern books. The rest of the court was not built till 1669, and is therefore a little later than the buildings at Clare, with which it has some affinity. Its western gateway and cloister form an excellent termination to the long perspective of St John's from the outer street. And the view of the court and library from the river is too well known to need remark.

Beyond the third court we are on modern ground. Mr Rickman's Bridge of Sighs is the beginning of the long cloister which forms one side of the New Court. The view from the bridge, including Ralph Symons' lovely Kitchen Bridge and the sweep of the Cam as it rounds the corner opposite Trinity Library, is more beautiful than the bridge itself; but the bridge, in its turn, is the most meritorious part of this immense court, in itself a college. It was built from Mr Rickman's designs between 1827 and 1831, and is a proof of the common criticism that its architect's theory was vastly superior to his practice. The extremely ornate cloister, with its traceried openings and vast central gateway, has no *raison d'être*, and the rest of the court is merely a huge barrack with a pretentious central staircase. From certain parts of the "Backs," when the shallow detail is sufficiently screened by trees, it forms an effective background to the prospect; but, near at hand, its effect is bare and ponderous.

Bridges of St. John's

All modern changes in the original buildings are to be found in the first court. In the original plan the Master's Lodge adjoined the Hall on the south, and the Chapel on the north, and filled up an angle between them. The court existed thus till 1774, when Essex came here, as to other colleges, and faced the south side with the present front, which might be creditable in Harley Street or Cavendish Square, but is merely ugly in a college. Further, in the early sixties, the College resolved to build a new chapel. The old one, whose site is marked by the slabs in the grass south of the existing chapel, was never a very remarkable building and was quite inadequate. So, in 1863, Sir Gilbert Scott came, built the chapel, and remodelled the court. The Master's Lodge was taken down, the Hall was lengthened by two bays, one of which is a new oriel, the staircase and lobby leading to the Combination Room were made, and the new Lodge was built on the ground north of the Library. Scott's immense chapel is, no doubt, too large for its purpose, and the heavy tower is painfully out of proportion to the rest, especially when seen from the west end. The style is typical of the architect's genius for imitation. He knew two buildings by heart, the Sainte Chapelle and the Angel Choir at Lincoln, and he put them into all his designs with a fatal formality. The exterior of St John's Chapel is somewhat tedious, and every detail is just a little too prominent—the statues in the buttresses, for example. On the whole, Scott's chapel at Exeter College, Oxford, is much better. But inside the building is very striking, especially the transeptal antechapel, which, in spite of the bad glass at the north end, recalls the antechapel of New College at Oxford. The tower inside is open to the first storey, and in the higher window there are good fragments of old glass. The glass in the inner chapel and in the great west window is by Clayton and Bell. Lord Powis, High Steward of the University at the time, gave the windows in the apse, and the rest are in memory of friends and benefactors of the college. The chapel was consecrated in 1869 by Dr Harold Browne, then Bishop of Ely. Some of the old stalls from the original chapel, with their miserere seats, have been kept; and the fine Early English piscina which belonged to the chapel of St John's Hospital has been incorporated in the arcading of the chancel. It belongs to a local class which includes the piscina at Jesus Chapel and the piscinae in the transepts at Histon, three miles away. Another relic is the altar tomb of Hugh Ashton, Archdeacon of York, who was one of the foundress' executors and died in 1522. The upper portion of the monument is canopied and richly coloured; the lower part is open and contains the "cadaver," which was fashionable with ecclesiastics of the day. Ashton's rebus, an ash growing out of a tun, appears in various parts of the base and canopy. In the antechapel also are Baily's statue of Dr Wood, Master of St John's and Dean of Ely, and the old altar-piece by Raphael Mengs. Other objects of interest are the paintings on the roof, a procession of illustrious Churchmen and Churchwomen of every age leading up to the figure of Our Lord in glory, which occupies the centre panel of the roof in the apse; the fine organ by Messrs Hill; and the marbles in the chancel. The chapel is 172 feet long and 63 feet high to the inner roof. The pitch of the outer roof is 80 feet, and the tower rises to 140 feet.

The Master's Lodge is a comfortable building, and contains a number of pictures, including two portraits of Charles I. and Henrietta Maria by Vandyck, and a large portrait of Matthew Prior (Rigaud) in his official robes. Since then, the only addition of structural importance to this interesting college has been the wing known as the Chapel Court, which runs at right angles to the main building opposite the west door of the chapel. This was added in 1884, by Mr F. C. Penrose, and is of red brick with white stone dressings and with a louvre in the centre. The college grounds have been laid out from time to time, and, with their winding walks and beautiful Fellow's Garden, are the most interesting and romantic of all the gardens near the river.

In founding St John's College, Lady Margaret Beaufort followed the precedent of Bishop Alcock. It is curious to observe how the most fervent Catholics of the Renaissance era subordinated monasticism to the revived learning and disestablished religious houses on merely nominal pretexts. The close likeness between the document which explains the dissolution of St Rhadegund's Nunnery and that which excused the abolition of St John's Hospital detracts from the value of the charges they contain and leads us to believe that they are merely repetitions of a recognised form. St John's Hospital was a small religious alms-house which had been founded in 1135 by one Henry Frost, and was under the management of Black Canons. It had a certain importance as being the first site of Hugh de Balsham's collegiate scheme. He grafted his scholars upon the monastic stock, but his plan was anything but a success, and he removed his *protégés* to Peterhouse. The hospital was not a very flourishing affair, and, whether the charges of immorality were true or not, there was sufficient excuse for its dissolution in the fact that in 1509 it contained only two brethren. The Lady Margaret, in that same year, the year of her own and her son's death, obtained leave to suppress it and found a college on its site. She had been prompted to this work by her confessor and faithful adviser, John Fisher, Bishop of Rochester, himself a man of great distinction in the University, a friend of learned men and a patron of study. And, although the college is very justly proud of its royal foundress and shares her coat-of-arms with Christ's College, the active part of the work was carried out by Fisher as her executor. The Charter of foundation was granted by Henry VIII. in 1511, and Fisher himself consecrated the Chapel in 1516. It follows that, although Fisher was a member of Queens' College, his name is connected almost entirely with St John's. This close relation of one man to two colleges is clearly manifested by the likeness which those parts of St John's built by Fisher's instrumentality bear to parts of Queens' College.

St John's College was the last and greatest of the Lady Margaret's works. When we think of the benefits which she conferred on Oxford and Cambridge, her noble provisions for the theological schools of both Universities, and her two foundations in Cambridge, we can only echo the words of the funeral sermon preached by Fisher in her honour, that the "students of both Universities, to whom she was as a mother ... for her death had cause of weeping." Very few colleges have so tender an attachment to a founder's memory as that which St John's has for Lady Margaret's; there are very few colleges which are so haunted, as it were, by their founder's spirit. And the history of St John's is a record worthy of the Lady Margaret. Although, in after years, it was a little overshadowed by the greater glory of

Trinity, it kept the second place against all competitors, and its roll of illustrious names is almost as crowded as that of Trinity itself.

The first master was Robert Shorton, who continued in the college for five years, after which time he became Master of Pembroke. His portrait is to be found among the great collection in the Master's Lodge. The early masters of the college followed one another very rapidly; in fact, between 1511 and 1612 we find no less than seventeen names, an almost unique instance of quick succession. Under the Tudors, too, the college history is not profoundly interesting. It is evident that, during the reign of Edward VI., the fashionable Genevan doctrines became popular in the college. Thomas Leaver, master in 1551, was a supporter of the new religion, and was, of course, ejected by Mary. However, with Elizabeth's reign the Puritan spirit returned in double force. The two Pilkingtons, who occupied the mastership in succession, introduced their Genevan and German friends to the Universities, and sought to model University life upon the system followed by the foreign Calvinists. It is worthy of remark that while, during this period, Trinity was producing Bacon, St John's had already produced the great Burghley, the first of her illustrious sons, and perhaps the most illustrious of them all. St John's became for many years the hereditary college of the Cecil family. The connection between the college and both branches of that great house is still kept up in the prize exercise known as the "Burghley Verses," one copy of which is sent annually to Hatfield and another to Burghley.[7]

The accession of noble families to the college and the consequent growth of court influence probably weaned the foundation from its Puritanism. Dr Whitaker* was the last of the Genevan School. He was a married man, and kept up an establishment for his wife in the town. The college prospered exceedingly in his time. These were the days of Dr Nevile of Trinity, when Cambridge received her most beautiful buildings. Whitaker's successor, Dr Richard Clayton, who ruled from 1595 to 1612, had the felicity of seeing the second court built under his auspices. Among the fellows at this time were Richard Neile,* and Thomas Morton,* who, as Archbishop of York and Bishop of Durham, were great benefactors to the college. And, with the reign of James I., the college began to distinguish itself, like St John the Baptist's College at Oxford, as a Royalist institution. Thomas Wentworth, Earl of Strafford,* the great Lord Lieutenant of Ireland, and Lucius Cary, Viscount Falkland,* the blameless hero of the Cavalier party, are the celebrities of the first half of the seventeenth century. In William Beale,* master from 1633 to 1644, the King had an enthusiastic supporter. In his time the college plate was melted down, and many valuable pieces were sacrificed. The plate was sent across country to Charles, who was then at York or Nottingham, and the passage was so well contrived that the convoy escaped the ambush set by Oliver Cromwell. Dr Beale was less happy, for Cromwell, in a fury, marched upon Cambridge, and took him prisoner while he was at his prayers in chapel. In company with Dr Martin of Queens' and Dr Sterne of Jesus, he was taken off to London and imprisoned in

[7] There is a somewhat untrustworthy tradition that Ben Jonson was a member of the college for a very short time. His means, although aided by the generosity of a friend, did not allow him to stay at Cambridge. Barry Cornwall supposed him to have been here or at Trinity.

the Tower. He died in 1646. During the Commonwealth, the college was ruled by Dr Arrowsmith and Dr Tuckney, but at the Restoration the famous divine, Dr Peter Gunning,* became master, having been previously Master of Corpus. He was made Bishop of Ely in 1670, when he was succeeded by Francis Turner.* In course of time, Turner succeeded Gunning at Ely. With these prelates we may couple the name of Edward Stillingfleet,* the well-known Bishop of Worcester.

Thomas Baker,* the historian of St John's College, deserves honourable mention. The treasure which Oxford possesses in Anthony Wood, St John's finds in Baker, whose accurate history, quaintly and piously written, is a mine of information on the subject of Cambridge life during the seventeenth century. Baker was a Royalist of considerable bias and a non-juror, in consequence of which he lost his fellowship. He was careful to describe himself on his title-page as *Socius Ejectus,* and gloried in the distinction. He died in 1740 at the age of eighty-four. His devotion to his college, not only to the foundation itself, but to its remotest benefactors, is a quality unique even in those days of fidelity to a principle. He set the college an example by which it has profited. To-day no college in Cambridge is in possession of such an amount of printed historical matter. Professor Mayor's monumental edition of Baker and of the life of Ambrose Bonwicke stand at the head of the list. Mr Torry's extremely full and interesting notes on the roll of Founders and Benefactors are invaluable, while Mr Scott's "Notes from the College Records," which are published from time to time in the college magazine, form a supplement and commentary to Baker's history. Ambrose Bonwicke, whose life is at once an exhortation to the painful student and a faithful picture of social life at Cambridge, entered St John's in 1710, the last year of the mastership of Turner's successor, Humphrey Gower. Bonwicke died early, so that the story of his labours and exertions, phenomenal in a mere boy and impossible in our own age, has a vivid pathos. From the light which he throws upon college life of his time, we are led to imagine that, however luxurious it may have been then, it would now be insupportable, if conducted in the same way. But then the prime object of university life was study, and athletics and dinner-parties were considered foreign to the main purpose.

Matthew Prior,* although a man of a different type from Baker, felt something of the same attachment for St John's. He was sent to Cambridge by his patron, the Earl of Dorset, and in course of time obtained a fellowship. With considerable forethought, he refused to give up his fellowship when promoted to high offices of state, and consequently, after his imprisonment by the Whigs in 1715 and the loss of all his fortune, he managed to keep body and soul together at Cambridge. The enormous portrait of him by Rigaud, which is now in the Master's Lodge, displays him in his robes as an ambassador, and is one of the most striking pictures in the college. He left a very beautiful collection of books to the library, among which may be mentioned a splendid folio edition of Ronsard's poems. His poetry is essentially of the outer world and not of Cambridge, but its culture and the academic flavour which is apparent in the most frivolous pieces bear clear testimony to the influence of the University on this light-hearted scholar. A very opposite type of scholarship—the laborious and critical—is represented by Richard Bentley,* who was a member of the society at the same time with Matthew Prior, and rose to further fame as Master of Trinity. In this period, too, Divinity was well represented. To say nothing of Bishops Gunning and Turner, great names in the history of theology, three masters of the college held, with their mastership, the Lady Margaret Professorship of Divinity within a very short time of each other. These were Dr Humphrey Gower,* master in 1679, Dr Robert Jenkin,* in 1711, and Dr Newcome in 1735.

Since the arrest of Dr Beale, St John's has enjoyed a very quiet history. In the eighteenth century, it produced the regulation number of noblemen and paid its full contribution to the cabinets of the period. Towards the end of the century, we remark the name of the eccentric Samuel Parr, whose portrait hangs in the Combination Room, and of Herbert Marsh (* Ponsford), the controversialist and Bishop of Peterborough, to whom Professor Mayor has devoted a large space in his edition of Baker's History. At the same time, we notice with interest that William Wilberforce (* G. Richmond) and Thomas Clarkson (* Room) were at St John's together, and, while there, doubtless cultivated the humanitarianism which is their common title to fame. Clarkson was a native of Cambridgeshire, having been born at Wisbech, where his father was master of the Grammar School, in 1760. But, in 1787, St John's received her most distinguished poet, William Wordsworth (* Pickersgill). He himself, in lines which are at once oddly prosaic and incomparably sublime, has described his impressions during his residence at Cambridge. These, however, are the sole tie which binds him to the place; for his retiring nature led him very little into society, and his emotions and impressions were all highly subjective. He has told us where his rooms were, but, owing to constant alterations, their exact position has been somewhat disputed. They are at present turned into one of the kitchen store-rooms. Some people, by a curious misreading of the text, have imagined that he could look into Trinity antechapel from his rooms and see Newton's statue. As a matter of fact, he merely says that he could see the antechapel, and this feat is easily performed from any back-window on the south side of the first court. Like most highly imaginative poets, and unlike the materialistic Matthew Prior, Wordsworth was a dilatory student, and he deserted Cambridge in 1791 for the wilder excitement of the French Revolution.

It is probable that no one has derived so much earthly benefit from an early death as Henry Kirke White, who entered the college in 1804, died in 1806, and has ever since been reckoned as one of its chief ornaments. He is also the only member of the University who has a public monument in Cambridge. At the age of nineteen he was a very promising mathematician, and was patronised by Southey as a rising poet. The small collection of poems and letters which constitute his "remains" show great religious fervour and some metrical skill, but their imagination is defective and morbid. His death excited great compassion, and his name still lives, in England and America, as that of a precocious genius. It is not unlikely that the greater name of Henry Martyn* is less widely known. This distinguished scholar and Orientalist became a fellow in 1802, but left Cambridge three years later to become a missionary. His life, short although it is, is a splendid record of devoted piety and self-denial. He went through dangers and privations in parts of the East which were then totally unknown to Europeans, and died in the prosecution of his labours. He may be regarded as the forerunner of a great band of Cambridge missionaries, the earliest name in a kalendar which includes Ragland, Mackenzie, Patteson and Smythies.

During the Napoleonic wars, Cambridge was possessed with a great martial ardour, and among the most active promoters of the volunteer movement of those days was Lord Temple,* who occupied rooms in the first court, looking out on the street. Later on, this nobleman was better known as Lord Palmerston. One of those who enrolled themselves under his guidance was that eccentric gentleman, Patrick Brontë, subsequently Vicar of Haworth in Yorkshire and father of a family whose tragic history is well known to every student of English literature. With the name of Palmerston, we touch modern times and come to the days of the scientific and mathematical pre-eminence of the college. An extraordinary number of great men have come from St John's during the present reign. Among scholars, Benjamin Hall Kennedy (* Ouless) has the first place. He was, before his election to the Greek professorship, Head Master of Shrewsbury, a school which has always been closely connected with St John's. The most distinguished historian was the late Charles Merivale, Dean of Ely, whose *History of the Romans under the Empire* is a monument of Cambridge scholarship. The names of scientists are legion, but one must not fail to mention John Couch Adams,* who was a Johnian and a fellow of the college. The late James Joseph Sylvester (* Emslie), although his genius was devoted to Oxford, is another man of world-wide fame whom St John's owns. The college supplied another distinguished professor to Oxford in the person of Charles Pritchard, the well-known Savilian professor. It is also necessary to mention the name of Edward Henry Palmer, Lord Almoner's Reader in Arabic, who, with one possible exception, was the best Oriental scholar of the century. More intimately related to the college were the two Babingtons, Churchill and Charles Cardale,* who spent their lives at Cambridge and filled University professorships. It would be invidious to select names of living members of the college, but Professor Mayor, (* Herkomer) the editor of Juvenal, and the present Bishop of Gloucester, Dr Ellicott, have their position securely assured. Recently, too, the death of the Hon. Charles Pelham Villiers, the "father of the House of Commons," robbed the college of an old member and constant friend. The modern history of St John's is essentially progressive, and, under Dr Bateson and the present master, Dr Taylor, the college has been worked on broad and liberal lines. Its yearly position in the schools testifies that it has in no way declined from its original purpose, and is still that nursery of learning which its foundress intended it to be. And, in connection with the modern development of the college, it is impossible not to say something of the College Mission. St John's was the first Cambridge college which thought of extending its energies for the benefit of the poor in large towns, and its mission in a crowded part of Walworth was the example which moved other colleges and schools to do something of the same kind. The result is shown in the beautiful church and group of buildings which form the nucleus of the parish. No more effectual realisation than this could be found of the ideal of the foundress and Bishop Fisher, that their work should not merely be accomplished for its own benefit, but that in time to come, what they had done for their scholars, their scholars should do for others.

CHAPTER XV

MAGDALENE COLLEGE

Magdalene is changed very little since the days of Samuel Pepys. Its first court has been refaced with new-looking red brick, but the interior, with its luxuriant covering of ivy, is time-worn and venerable. There is, however, not much of any importance. The Hall is, perhaps, the best which is to be found among the smaller colleges, and the spacious double staircase which leads from it to the Combination Room, is a feature of which any college might justly be proud. "Although the staircase, as it exists, is the work of restorers, the detail of the woodwork is excellent, and was doubtless suggested by the fine Renaissance carving at Audley End." The Chapel, north of the court, was restored in 1847, and retains some of the ancient features, including the roof. There is some modern stained glass, not very good. Beyond the Hall, in the same position as the building at Christ's (with which it may be compared), is the famous Pepysian Library, a charming building in the very latest style of Renaissance Gothic. Its general effect is quite equal to the earlier work at Christ's, and is very superior to that of the river front at Clare, with which it is almost contemporary. The spandrils of the arches in the basement are very profusely decorated with fantastic patterns, and similar ornaments appear in the space between the library windows and the heavy cornice below them. The Ionic pilasters of the central compartment show traces of the Palladian influence which just then found its way everywhere; and it is a fortunate circumstance that the architect had enough feeling for his style not to multiply them. As it is, they add to the charm of the building, and bring its central division into a prominence which is demanded by the two very plain wings with their chimneyed gables and rusticated angles. The Master's Lodge (1835) is north of the college, and is supposed to stand on one of the escarpments of the ancient Camboritum—that is, if the Castle-Hill is Camboritum. Otherwise, it is a simple Gothic building, rather better than most houses of the time, but with no obtrusive features.

Magdalene College

We have seen that Jesus and St John's Colleges were founded by means of the dissolution of monastic houses. Magdalene, founded thirty-one years after St John's, was merely the final step in the secularisation of a religious house. In 1428 Henry VI. granted the site of the present college to the monks of Crowland, who wished to found a hostel at Cambridge for the use of their scholars at that University. The Abbeys of Ely, Ramsey and Walden joined with Crowland in the work, and contributed to the building. In the latter half of the century this theological college, as we should call it, received substantial aid from Henry Stafford, Duke of Buckingham, whose favours were continued in 1519 by his son Edward. In recognition of the benefactions of Duke Henry, the hostel took its title of Buckingham College. The foundation seems to have departed gradually from its original purpose, for laymen were admitted to it before the dissolution. However, it was only natural that, when Crowland surrendered to the King, its dependent house should surrender also. The crown resumed the property in December, 1539. Henry VIII. granted the messuages of Buckingham College to Thomas, Lord Audley of Walden, who also became possessed of Walden Abbey. In all probability, the original connection between the abbey and the college induced him to refound the institution on a new plan. He reconstituted it in 1542 under the name of the College of St Mary Magdalene. Since his day, through all the vicissitudes of his family, Magdalene College has remained under the protection and patronage of the owner of Audley End, a stately and beautiful appendage to the noblest country house in England. His work was carried on by his successors. At his death he left a daughter, the lady whose magnificent portrait by Lucas van Heere hangs in the great hall at Audley End. She married the Duke of Norfolk, who, in 1564, being at Cambridge with Queen Elizabeth, generously promised the college an annuity of £40 until they had finished the "quadrant of their college," and further endowed the society, which was become much impoverished, with landed property. Norfolk's liberality was supplemented by the contributions of the Lord Chief Justice Sir Christopher Wray,* who had been one of the lay students of Buckingham College.

The college was never large, and its history is scanty. Its first master of any importance was Dr Thomas Nevile, who reigned from 1582 to 1593, and then removed to Trinity. His fame belongs to the history of the latter college. In the great concussion of the seventeenth century, Magdalene adhered, as was natural, to the royalist side, and its master, Dr Rainbow,* was rewarded after the Restoration with the Bishoprick of Carlisle. Nicholas Ferrar,* the famous superior of the community at Little Gidding, and the friend of Crashaw and Herbert, was a member of this college as well as of Clare, and his portrait, with that of his mother, is preserved in the Master's Lodge. This saintly man, like Herbert, was happy in dying before the troubles of his party began. But one naturally connects Magdalene less with Ferrar than with an individual of a very different order. Mr Samuel Pepys was entered at Trinity in 1650, but, for some reason, preferred Magdalene. By no means a scholar, he enjoyed the social advantages of the University, and in after years remembered the grateful flavour of Goody Mulliner's stewed prunes, which he used to buy "over against the college." His eventual generosity to Magdalene was something of an accident. During the closing years of his life, the college was raising the exquisite eastern building. Pepys was then casting about for a suitable destination for his library, and there is no doubt that the singularly admirable qualities of the new building, as well as his own prepossession for Magdalene, aided his decision. By his will, he bequeathed his library to his nephew, Mr Jackson (another Magdalene man), as his trustee, and provided that, at the death of this gentleman, it should pass to Magdalene, and, by an express stipulation, be housed in the New Building "and any part thereof, at my nephew's selection." The document contained certain reservations in favour of Trinity. Its whole wording shows an amusing caution. After a preamble, in which he expresses his apprehension of the danger which might befall the books at the hands of an incompetent heir, he proceeds to leave them, at his nephew's death, to one of the two Universities, but to Cambridge rather than to Oxford. Then he states his preference for a private to a public library, and confines the private libraries to Trinity and Magdalene. Finally, he prefers Magdalene to Trinity, but provides that, in case of specified losses, the books are forfeit to the latter college. In this respect, he imitates Parker's bequest to Corpus. "And that for a yet further security herein, the s^{d} two colleges of Trinity and Magdalen have a reciprocall check upon one another; and that college, wch shall be in present possession of the s^{d} Library, be subject to an annual visitation from the other, and to the forfeiture thereof, to the like possession and use of the other, upon conviction of any breach of their s^{d} covenants."

John Jackson died in 1724, and the precious legacy passed to Magdalene. Its value is incontestable, and no treasure is to this day more jealously guarded. The inscription "Bibliotheca Pepysiana," and Pepys' motto, "Mens cujusque is est quisque," were put up on the building after the arrival of the books. The value of the bequest was more fully illustrated when, in the present century, Lord Braybrooke, a Magdalene man himself and visitor of the college, translated Pepys' cypher diary and gave that unvarnished picture of contemporary manners to the world, opening thereby a most fruitful mine of research, as well as discovering a hidden classic. Dr Peter Peckard,* master from 1781 to 1797, enriched the library with his own collection. He was Dean of Peterborough. The see of Peterborough, at the beginning of the same century, was held by a Magdalene man, Dr Richard Cumberland, whose very exhaustive treatise on Jewish Weights and Measures, as well as his polemical essay in answer to Hobbes, are still remembered, although seldom read. The name of Daniel Waterland,* master from 1713 to 1746, is of greater fame in the history of controversial theology.

The present century, from 1813 to the present day, is covered by the long masterships of an uncle and a nephew. The first of these was the Hon. George Neville Grenville, Dean of Windsor (* Pickersgill); the second is the present master, the Hon. Latimer Neville, who has ruled his college for forty-five years. The Nevilles of Audley End are descendants of the founder in the female line. The first Lord Braybrooke, the editor of Pepys' Diary, was a Neville of Billingsbear in Essex, and succeeded the last Lord Howard de Walden, of the family of Griffin, on the death of that nobleman without male issue. During the century, Magdalene has had some reputation as a fashionable college; but the amusing American critic, Mr Everett, spoke of it somewhat unjustly when he said that "it is a favourite home for young men who are of the opinion, either from conjecture or experience, that

CHAPTER XVI

TRINITY COLLEGE

The Great Court of Trinity represents the earlier foundations of King's Hall and Michael House. Of these, the latter was the older, and its buildings occupied a position nearly corresponding to the south-western angle of the present court. It may safely be supposed that, up to the last half of the eighteenth century, some remains of the original building were allowed to exist, although Dr Nevile had probably faced them in accordance with his general design. In 1771, however, James Essex made a radical alteration in this corner, and the only part which was thought worthy of preservation was the kitchen. This quaint room, entered by a passage from the hall-screens, still survives, and may be regarded as the nucleus of the modern Trinity. The next relic of importance is the King's Tower, which now blocks up the west end of the Chapel, and occupies the centre of the north side of the court. It stood originally a little south-east of its present site, and opened at the junction of two lanes, one of which ran diagonally from the old church of All Saints' to the Cam, while the other, coming from the present Trinity Lane, was bounded on the west by the small court of Michael House. Now, of course, the tower, removed and rebuilt, shows very little trace of antiquity, and the oldest part of it is the statue of Edward III., which stands above the gateway, and bears the inscription "Tertius Edwardus fama super aethera notus." This may be ascribed to the reign of Edward IV. Later on, in the reign of Henry VII., the foundation of the great gateway was laid, and a chapel for the scholars of King's Hall was built.

other colleges are too strict for them." It has, like other small colleges, produced an excellent percentage of scholars and learned men. Our opinions as to the literary merits of Charles Kingsley (* Lowes Dickinson) may be divided, but there can be no question as to his abiding influence on English letters. He is equally well known as parish priest, cathedral dignitary, novelist and poet, and Professor of Modern History. The roll of living members includes the name of Professor Alfred Newton (* Lowes Dickinson), and the genial and kindly influence of the late Mr Frank Pattrick (* Dickinson), Tutor and President of the college, is gratefully remembered by the latest and youngest of those who have pursued their studies at Magdalene.

Trinity College

Not long after King's Hall had received its new eastern gateway, which implies a considerable extension of the college, Henry VIII. dissolved the lesser foundations and founded Trinity as we know it. Henry's chief wish was to provide a sufficient chapel. It was not, however, until Mary's reign that any activity was shown in this work. Mary furthered her father's project, and allowed the builders to use the ruins of Cambridge Castle as their quarry. The work was finished by Elizabeth. Trinity Chapel is an excellent example of late Perpendicular work. As Gothic work, it is stiff and debased, and forms a striking contrast to the elegance of the Renaissance Hall. Its exterior has been very little altered. Internally, however, it belongs to a much later period. The west window was filled up by Nevile; the east window is obscured by a huge baldachino of the last century. During Bentley's mastership, Father Smith built the present organ, one of the largest in England; and the whole chapel was refitted to suit the capacities of this instrument. Opinions may differ about the beauty of the heavy wooden screen in an uncompromisingly classical taste which supports the organ and divides the chapel from the antechapel; but it is unquestionably a very appropriate addition to a stately, if ugly, interior. The carving of the stalls is by Grinling Gibbons. Alterations did not stop here. The present century has made the building what it is. Within the last thirty years the roof and walls have been highly decorated in accordance with the rest of the chapel, and the result is very imposing. Mr Henry Holiday's stained glass, which represents the saints and worthies of the Church from the earliest period, is good, although its merits are a little various. The western windows near the organ, devoted to members of Trinity, are the best. In the antechapel the glass is very bad indeed. Otherwise, this part of the building is not much altered, and its panelling of dark oak makes it one of the most impressive sights in either university. This is much increased by the fine statues. Of these, that of Newton, by Roubiliac, was given in 1755 by the master, Dr Smith. The rest are more modern. Bacon's statue, by Weekes, was given by Dr Whewell; Barrow's by the late Lord Lansdowne. The statues of Macaulay and Whewell are both by Woolner.

These various buildings and others which had grown about them were gathered together in the reign of James I., and the result is the Great Court, one of the largest and certainly without exception the most beautiful of quadrangles in the world. Trinity owes a great debt to Thomas Nevile, who was master from 1593 to 1615. To bring his buildings into a systematic form, he took down King Edward III.'s tower and rebuilt it west of the chapel. He added the upper storey to the great gateway, and placed the statue of Henry VIII. in a niche outside, while on the side towards the court he set up in corresponding niches statues of James I., Prince Charles, and the Princess Elizabeth. On the south side he built the Queen's tower, which contains the figure of Queen Mary, and is exactly opposite King Edward's tower. Finally, to the west he built the Hall, north of the old hall of Michael House, and, further north still, the Master's Lodge. His architect was that admirable genius, Ralph Symons. Although the Great Court has been partly faced with stucco and, in certain places, refronted, its beauty is indestructible. The sets of rooms which join the towers and other buildings together, have their height in very just proportion to the size of the quadrangle. What the effect would be, were they higher than they are, may be seen by comparing the Jacobean buildings with Essex's classical addition near the kitchen, and the modern Gothic buildings between the Chapel and Lodge. The beauty of the court finds its central point, perhaps, in Nevile's exquisite fountain, built in 1602, which has all the best attributes of English Renaissance work. It may be compared with the gateway just outside the south-western corner of the court.

The Fountain, Trinity College

E·H·N

The Hall, with its light oriels and graceful louvre, was finished in 1604. Its interior is, perhaps, a little over-decorated, but possesses a certain splendour which finds no parallel in England. The western gallery, covered with rich carving and highly gilded, may be compared with the similar galleries at Audley End and other contemporary houses. The portraits are interesting, although of no great excellence as a whole. Newton, Bacon, and Barrow occupy the north end, and other celebrities, such as Dryden, Cowley and Pearson, are to be found on the side walls above the panelling. Sir Joshua Reynolds' charming portrait of the little Duke of Gloucester hangs close to the western oriel, and near it is Mr Watts' portrait of Tennyson. Other modern portraits are those of Thackeray (Lockhart Bogle), Dr Thompson (Herkomer), Dr Lightfoot (Richmond), and, of living celebrities, Professor Michael Foster (Herkomer) and Dr Henry Jackson (C. W. Furse).

Beyond the Hall, Nevile built the court, which bears his name, and, for a certain beauty of its own, is not far behind the Great Court. Ralph Symons was again his architect. This building consisted of two wings, shorter than at present, at right angles to the Hall, and built above a cloister. These splendid arcades are the very crown of Renaissance work in Cambridge; their cloistered ground-floor recalls Bologna or Padua rather than the court of an English university; but their upper stories are thoroughly English work. Nevile's Court did not assume its present secluded, aristocratic appearance until considerably more than a hundred years later. Isaac Barrow, one of the many great Masters of Trinity, began the library in 1675, with Sir Christopher Wren as his architect. The court was completed by the generous addition of two compartments to the original arcades, which was paid for by some of the fellows. Wren's Library is so prominent that its incongruity with the rest of the court is not at once obvious, but there can be no doubt that it is seen at its best on the river side. Its front towards the court is adorned with a bas-relief which represents the dedication of the Septuagint to Ptolemy Philadelphus. On the roof are four statues of learned nymphs by Gabriel Cibber, which are chiefly remarkable for the part they played in one of Byron's most senseless freaks. The interior of the Library is matchless for its magnificent simplicity. It is a pity that the arbiters of taste in the last century should have allowed Cipriani to design the window at the south end, but this is the sole fault. The numerous busts (some by Roubiliac), the carvings on the bookcases (Grinling Gibbons) and Thorwaldsen's statue of Byron are remarkable.

Wren is also supposed to have harmonised the side of the Hall which stands opposite, with his Library. The present meaningless alcoves and the balustrade which have superseded Nevile's work on this side, are probably by Essex, who was brought in to prop up the Hall and build the Combination Room and Kitchen Offices in 1771. A little while before Wren began working at Trinity, John Hacket, Bishop of Lichfield and Coventry, founded Bishop's Hostel, the small building south of the Great Court, and close to the Trinity Lane entrance. These buildings (1670) are now somewhat overlapped by the modern buildings of Garret Hostel, which are also of red brick. Garret Hostel is, however, a much older component of Trinity, and the modern buildings are simply a revival.

During the eighteenth century Bentley effected his famous alterations in the

Lodge and Chapel, and Essex made the additional changes to which I have referred. No actual addition was made to the college until, in 1823, William Wilkins began his court in the revived Gothic taste, adjoining Nevile's Court on the south. George IV. proved a benefactor to the extent of £1000, and the official name of the new building is for this reason King's Court. It was finished about six years later. Cambridge, as we have seen, has a long tale to tell of Georgian Gothic, and the New Court of Trinity is a very typical example of that period. It nevertheless is a far more pleasant building than Wilkins' court at Corpus or Rickman's at St John's, although there is not much to praise in it. To a much better period of modern Gothic belong Mr Beresford Hope's improvements in the Lodge and the Master's Courts, usually known as Whewell's Court (and by more familiar names), which are opposite the great gate of Trinity, and are one of the thoroughfares between Trinity Street and Sidney Street. Dr Whewell built this court at his own expense, with Salvin as his architect. Outside, it is gloomy but imposing. The darkness of its interior was till quite recently almost to be felt; but now (1898) they are being refaced, and the depressing rooms are being made into comfortable and picturesque habitations.

The grounds of Trinity are spacious and pleasant, and the famous lime-walk is one of the wonders of Cambridge. When Dr Nevile built his court, he filled up a branch of the Cam which ran northwards from Garret Hostel Bridge and rejoined the main stream at the north-west corner of the present Library. The bridge which connects the lime-walk with the new court was built by Essex, and is his best work in Cambridge, if that is any praise.

The royal foundation of Trinity College is, as a matter of fact, one of the youngest colleges in Cambridge. At the same time, it is to Cambridge what Christ Church is to Oxford, and, more than that, its name, to a great number of people, is almost synonymous with Cambridge. Henry VIII., the most learned of our English sovereigns, was naturally a great patron of learning. In 1546, the year in which, with his characteristic want of scruple, he took upon himself the credit of founding Wolsey's great college at Oxford, he also founded Trinity at Cambridge. His material was ready to hand, for the small colleges and hostels which filled up the space between the present Trinity Street and the river provided scanty room for their members, and needed amalgamation. Trinity, in fact, as it now exists, is composed of a number of separate foundations, the principal of which were Michael House, founded in 1324, and King's Hall, founded by Edward III. in 1337. These two colleges had gradually absorbed many of the smaller hostels. The founder of Michael House was Hervé de Staunton, treasurer to King Edward II. In spite of its limited situation, it had a certain amount of prestige, and one of its last masters was John Fisher, afterwards President of Queens' and Bishop of Rochester. It used the church of St Michael as its chapel. King's Hall, on the other hand, had, by the time of Henry VIII., extended its boundaries and built its own chapel. It had grown out of a corporation of scholars, which had found a patron in Edward II., and had been presented by Edward III., in 1336, with a piece of ground belonging to one Robert of Crowland—which may point to a connection between the foundation and Crowland Abbey, the great centre of English learning. A regular charter was granted in 1337. The accounts of the institution remain, and point to a style of living which would not be very highly accounted of now, but was positively luxurious for medieval Cambridge. The scholars attended chapel at St Mary's by the Market and All Saints' in the Jewry, until, in Edward IV.'s reign, they obtained leave to found a chapel for themselves. King's Hall naturally became the nucleus of Henry's college, and the lesser buildings found their centre in its court, enlarged and beautified. John Redman, the last master of King's Hall, became the first master of Trinity College.

Under the charter of 1546, Henry VIII. founded Trinity College for a master and sixty fellows and scholars. The full title was "Trinity College within the Town and University of Cambridge of King Henry the Eighth's foundation." Michael House, dedicated primarily to St Michael the Archangel, had been founded under the secondary invocations of the Holy and Undivided Trinity, St Mary, and All Saints; and it is probable that the first of these suggested the name under which the college has become so famous. Trinity College is the most distinguished fruit of that revived learning which paved the way for and accompanied the Reformation: from the very beginning its tendencies were liberal and progressive; every genius which it nourished was eminently constructive. The names of its three greatest *alumni*, Newton, Bacon, and Barrow, form, so to speak, the three fountain-heads of organized philosophical thought in England; and there are a hundred less monumental names which are sufficient guarantee of the intellectual supremacy of Trinity over her sisters. The history of the college divides itself naturally into periods. The first is a period of consolidation, extending from 1546 to 1593. During this time, the college suffered the ordinary vicissitudes of the Reformation. Its chapel, which had been projected by Henry VIII., was begun by Mary and finished, probably out of a sense of duty, by Elizabeth. In 1553, William Bill, the second master, who had been appointed under Edward VI., had to retire in favour of a Catholic master, John Christopherson, but was of course restored at the accession of Elizabeth. He was succeeded in 1561 by Robert Beaumont, who presented to the Master's Lodge a portrait of the founder by Lucas van Heere, one of the most excellent portrait-painters of the sixteenth century. Beaumont, in his turn, was succeeded by John Whitgift, who was already well known in Cambridge as Master of Peterhouse and Pembroke, and Fellow of Queens'. Whitgift, with Matthew Parker and Matthew Hutton, is one of the three divines who may be taken as typical of Elizabethan Cambridge—strongly anti-papal in their sentiments, but keeping nevertheless a cautious eye on the political balance. It is hardly necessary to add that Whitgift's long list of Cambridge preferments eventually led to the Archbishoprick of Canterbury. And it was during his mastership that the greatest intellect of the age was trained at his college. Under the yoke of the Aristotelian system of philosophy, Francis Bacon, while still at Cambridge, perceived the fallacies of the stereotyped methods of thought, and laid the foundation of inductive science. Bacon's life is connected more intimately with affairs of state than with his University; but Trinity regards him as one of the principal saints in her kalendar, and his memory greets the visitor at every turn. His portrait is one of the three at the end of the Hall; there is another in the Master's Lodge; his bust, by Roubiliac, is in the Library; and, in 1845, his statue was placed, side by side with that of Newton, in the antechapel.

Bacon is the great figure of this early period. Nine years older than he, the Lord Chief Justice Coke (* Whood: bust by Roubiliac) is the first of the great lawyers connected with Trinity. Another celebrated name is that of Dr Donne, Dean of St Paul's, divine and poet. Sir Henry Spelman (* Whood), the antiquary and translator of Xenophon, was a contemporary of Bacon, and, some years after, Sir Robert Cotton (* bust by Roubiliac) furnished Trinity with another archæologist. Whitgift, after his translation to Canterbury, was succeeded by John Still, who became Bishop of Bath and Wells. With Still's successor, Dr Thomas Nevile,* master from 1593 to 1615, the second period opens. Nevile held the Deanery of Canterbury with his mastership, but his life was spent in Cambridge, and his architectural work in Trinity, while it is the most important in the University, stamps him as the chief benefactor of the college. In that great age of building, Nevile's work has an honourable pre-eminence: it is the sign of a monumental perseverance and an artistic taste which, even in that fine era of Renaissance culture, was never surpassed. We may with justice echo the words of Fuller, who says that Dr Nevile performed this work "answering his anagram *most heavenly*, and practising his own allusive motto *ne vile velis*." Higher praise could not be given. Nevile's buildings, if architecture may be considered to reflect contemporary history, may be regarded as a turning-point in Cambridge thought. When we look at the reactionary tendency to the Gothic taste in Jacobean Oxford, and compare it with the distinct preference shown in Cambridge for classical and Renaissance models, the radical divergence of the two Universities is clear. Nevile's courts at Trinity were the beginning of a long series of collegiate buildings which, often very defective, took the place of Gothic work and held it for the next two centuries. The sole exception to this rule is Matthew Wren's chapel at Peterhouse. Besides his building energy, Nevile acquired land for the college, so that, when the Society enlarged its buildings in after years, it found itself in possession of the requisite site. The King's Court occupies part of this property. One can only say that Nevile's memory might be honoured with a better building.

One of the first scholars of Trinity who saw Nevile's work in its complete state was George Herbert. He was born in 1593, the first year of Nevile's mastership, and entered Trinity at a very early age. Although it is more natural to think of him as a parish priest and the writer of the most beautiful devotional poetry in English, his career at Cambridge was not without distinction. His early Latinity was as perfect as Milton's, and he filled the office of Public Orator of the University. He is unique among Trinity men as the only important member of the college who belonged to the most illustrious school of English churchmen—the school which, under Andrewes, Laud and Cosin, placed the Church of England on a logical and independent footing. The honours of this school are shared rather unequally between the two Universities, but Cambridge contributed a substantial quota to the whole sum. There is no portrait of Herbert in the college, but he is commemorated in one of the chapel windows. He died at the early age of forty, before the troubles of the Great Rebellion. John Hacket,* the Royalist Bishop of Lichfield and Coventry, was probably at Trinity with Herbert. He is remembered, not so much for his divinity as for his gallant defence of his cathedral against the Puritan destroyers. He was born in 1592 and did not die till 1670, ten years after the Restoration. In his seventieth year, having been mercifully preserved throughout the troubles, he desired to bestow some mark of his affection upon Trinity, "that Society," as he said with a noble pathos characteristic of the party to which he had attached himself, "which is more precious to me, next to the Church of Jesus Christ, than any place upon earth." The result of his bequest was the present Bishop's Hostel, which occupied part of the site of the old Garret's or Gerrard's Hostel.

The seventeenth century is fertile in great men. During the century, however, none of the masters of the college were very conspicuous men, and the mastership, between 1615 and 1683, changed hands no less than twelve times. It is also worthy of remark that three successive masters ended their lives as Bishops of Chester, thus uniting Henry VIII.'s collegiate foundation with one of his bishopricks. These were John Wilkins (* Whood), master in 1659, Henry Ferne, master in 1660, and John Pearson (* Whood), master from 1662 to 1673. This last is the only exception to the general insignificance of the masters at this time. He was a distinguished scholar who had been connected with several colleges, and had held the mastership of Jesus. His work on the Apostles' Creed is still one of the classics of English theology. About the middle of the century, Dryden (* Hudson) came to Trinity from Westminster School. Both he and Abraham Cowley (* Slaughton) were strongly attached to the Royalist side during the Commonwealth disturbances, and Cowley, who entered the college in 1637 and proceeded to his master's degree, was expelled in 1643 on account of his too strongly expressed loyalty. He found more congenial soil at St John's College, Oxford, the college of Laud, Juxon, and others of the same party. If to these poets we add the names of the naturalists Ray (* Hudson: bust by Roubiliac) and Willoughby (bust by Roubiliac) we shall have enumerated the most illustrious Trinity men of their time. Ray and Willoughby, who studied natural history with special reference to its religious character, were, in fact, the founders of the modern science, just as Dryden may be said to have struck the first note of modern poetry.

Pearson became Bishop of Chester in 1672, and removed there in 1673. Under his successor, Isaac Barrow, began the golden age of Trinity. Barrow is, in many ways, the most extraordinary genius of whom Cambridge can boast. He was one of that rare class whose knowledge is practically universal. He was born in 1630, a year before his great contemporary, John Locke, who went up to Oxford from Westminster about the time when Barrow went up from Charterhouse to Cambridge. Barrow was a man of surprising energy and, at Cambridge, he appears to have read deeply in every subject which was then studied. He was classic, mathematician, scientist, theologian, and orator; and in each of these branches he excelled. He was appointed Regius Professor of Greek in 1655, and, subsequently, Lucasian Professor of Mathematics—a feat which, to the scholars of to-day, would seem next to impossible. Undoubtedly, however, his promotion to the mastership of his college and his subsequent celebrity were due to his fame as a divine. His sermons bear the same relation to his age that those of Jeremy Taylor bear to the

Stewart period. He was in high favour as a preacher at court, and, on Pearson's retirement, his appointment was obvious. He did not hold the mastership for more than four years, as in 1677 he died at the age of forty-seven. His portrait by Hudson hangs in the college Hall; his bust, by Roubiliac, is in the Library; and his statue, by Noble, was placed in the antechapel during the mastership of his worthy successor, Whewell.

At this time, the mathematical attainments of the Society must have been overpowering. Barrow's fame in this department has perhaps been obscured by that of Sir Isaac Newton; but, if we are to believe Newton's generous compliment, the early death of Roger Cotes robbed Trinity of an even greater prodigy. The college may nevertheless be well content with Newton, who was emphatically a Trinity man, spending very little of his life away from Cambridge. He was twelve years younger than Barrow, and entered Trinity in the year of the Restoration, when he was eighteen. Nine years later, his studies proved so fruitful that Barrow gave up the Lucasian professorship in his favour. For more than half a century, he was the chief ornament of the University. His discoveries revolutionised the whole theory of mathematics, and it was owing to his personality that the subsequent energies of Cambridge were so largely mathematical. He occupied rooms between the Great Gateway and the Chapel. Although he made Cambridge his home, he had a large share in public business, sitting as Member for the University and receiving the mastership of the Mint. This office he probably owed to another member of the college, Charles Montague, Earl of Halifax (* Kneller), whose recall of the specie is among the most famous of English financial operations. In 1703, Newton was elected President of the Royal Society, which, it is interesting to note, had been founded, forty years before, mainly through the energy of Dr Wilkins, Master of Trinity and one of the three Bishops of Chester mentioned above. Newton was knighted by Queen Anne in 1705, and died in 1727. His scientific studies were not his exclusive pursuits, for he was, to a certain extent, one of the group of literary men who are the glory of Anne's reign, and was also much occupied with the elucidation of prophecy, which probably attracted him from its mathematical side. Trinity has very justly regarded him as her greatest son. His portrait, by Ritz, occupies the place of honour in the Hall, and every visitor to Cambridge knows—

> The antechapel where the statue stood
> Of Newton with his prism and silent face,
> The marble index of a mind for ever
> Voyaging through strange seas of Thought, alone.

The statue, which is by Roubiliac, and is that master's most famous work, bears the inscription from Lucretius "Qui genus humanum ingenio superavit." There is a bust of him in the Library, also by Roubiliac, and several portraits are to be found throughout the college.

After Barrow's death, the mastership was filled successively by the Hon. John North* and the Hon. John Montague,* whose rule was calculated to foster a comfortable laziness rather than industry. On the death of the second of these, Dr Richard Bentley, fellow of St John's, was elected master. There was, in those days, a strong feeling of rivalry between the two foundations—not only academical, but also in political and social matters. Bentley was a rare genius, whose scholarship was just then acknowledged as the finest in England, but he was utterly devoid of good feeling and tact, and had a peculiar faculty for exciting hatred. His fame, for the most of us, is due to his high place in the *Dunciad*. He arrived in Trinity with the intention of managing the college on his own lines. There was a party in the Society which thoroughly enjoyed the comfort of a position it did not adorn, and in this body Bentley found his most devoted enemies. Instead of conciliating them, he treated them with undisguised contempt and arrogance; and his conduct was so injudicious that he alienated all the better members of the college from himself. Matters came to a head when Bentley made radical alterations in the Master's Lodge, and presented the fellows with a bill considerably larger than the original estimate. Open war broke out; the fellows refused to pay; and Bentley in consequence applied methods of coercion, withholding privileges which were in his gift. The fellows found themselves obliged to give in after some time, and Bentley followed up this victory by altering the interior of the chapel to suit the new organ. At this point, however, the Society revolted for good. Bentley required a large subscription of each fellow. The fellowship dividends had been much reduced during the previous years, and, with this additional burden, poverty stared many of the dons in the face. In this crisis, the fellows, who undoubtedly had justice on their side, called in Serjeant Milne, a London lawyer and one of their number, and, under his guidance, addressed a *gravamen* against the Master to the Bishop of Ely. Things would have gone hardly for Bentley, had not the Bishop died opportunely. This Bishop, by the way, was John Moore, whose books George I. gave to the University Library. However, Bentley's tyranny was not suffered to continue, for, in 1718, the Senate passed a grace degrading him from his high positions in the University. After this, the quarrel was less prominent. Bentley occupied the Lodge till 1742, but the bad feeling which he had excited continued till the end of his life. His judgment and taste may be estimated from the reply which he is said to have given to some congratulatory address after his election. Referring to his original college of St John's, he said, "By the help of my God, I have leaped over a wall." His arrogance might have been excusable in a young man whose promotion was early, but Bentley, in 1700, was past middle life. His scholarship was sound, and there is no doubt that his arguments against the Epistles of Phalaris crushed the position of his adversary Boyle; but his lack of proper feeling always put him in the wrong, and his memory lives in the satire of Pope and Swift rather than in his own work. Hudson's portrait of him is in the Hall, and his bust, by Roubiliac, is in the Library.

The quarrels of Bentley's mastership form a period by themselves in the college history. At the same time, it must be remembered that the quarrel was confined to a section of the Society, and that the better members kept aloof from it. It had nevertheless a marked effect on the college throughout the eighteenth century, with the consequence that famous names are comparatively scanty. Of Bentley's opponents, the most distinguished was Dr Conyers Middleton, whose life of Cicero was good enough to merit a century of abuse. Lesser scholars of the same time were Roger Gale,* the antiquary, who is often confounded with the learned Theophilus Gale of Magdalen, Oxford, author of the once famous *Court of* *the Gentiles;* and Beaupré Bell* of Outwell, Norfolk, who was an enthusiastic lover of church architecture, and left his valuable manuscripts to the college library. Bentley's immediate successor, Dr Robert Smith,* master from 1742 to 1768, bequeathed his name to the Smith's Prizes. He was succeeded by John Hinchliffe, Bishop of Peterborough, a typical prelate of the last century and a born pluralist. Lord Orford, in his *Tour of the Fens,* describes his entertainment at the Palace of Peterborough; from which we may divine that Hinchliffe was fond of a good dinner and liked the vicinity of a nobleman. On one occasion, he put a man with no voice into the Trinity choir, because he happened to have a vote for Peterborough. A fellow of the college, named Mansel, who was more remarkable for his ponderous wit than his piety, wrote the following epigram:—

A singing man, and yet not sing?
How justify your patron's bounty?
Forgive me; you mistake the thing;
My voice is in another county.

This same Mansel* came, some years later, to great dignity as Bishop of Bristol and Master of Trinity. His mastership, from 1798 to 1820, closes the eighteenth century. The most distinguished member of the college at this time was the great Professor of Greek, Richard Porson,* who died in 1808 at the age of forty-nine. His beautiful Greek handwriting may be seen in one of the cases in the college library. Otherwise, the scholars of the last century are few and far between. Trinity was, however, the great nursing-place for noblemen; and among the number of her sons may be mentioned the famous Marquess of Granby (* Reynolds) whose head serves as the sign for so many inns; John Jefferies Pratt, Marquess Camden and Chancellor of the University (* Lawrence), George Henry Fitzroy, Duke of Grafton (* Lawrence), and, of royal blood, William Frederick, Duke of Gloucester (* Gainsborough, Romney, Opie), Chancellor of the University, and Frederick Augustus, Duke of Sussex (* Lonsdale). A great statesman of the day was Spencer Perceval,* who was assassinated in the lobby of the Houses of Parliament. But, if we turn to men of letters and poets, we merely find such men as the parodist, Isaac Hawkins Browne.*

Lord Byron received his education under Mansel. His career at Cambridge would be scarcely worth recording, were he not Byron; for it is the record of a foolish series of silly exploits and eccentricities bordering on madness. The place of honour which is given to his statue in the library always seems a little better than his merits. He occupied rooms in Nevile's Court, and contrived, during his residence, to irritate the college authorities. Mansel, as master, had a very exalted idea of the virtues of his position, and, from the anecdotes which are told of him, must have made himself peculiarly unpleasant. He was the last master of Trinity who combined that office with episcopal dignity. His successor, Christopher Wordsworth,* master from 1820 to 1841, was brother to the poet, and father of the late saintly Bishop of Lincoln.

During Wordsworth's time, the college was full of great men. Adam Sedgwick* was Professor of Geology. Another member of the college was Thomas Babington Macaulay, who was born with the century. As Fellow of Trinity, the great historian was thoroughly identified with the college, and, nine years after his death, his statue, by Woolner, was placed among the distinguished society of the antechapel. Younger by nine years than Macaulay was Alfred Tennyson (* Watts), who, in a few exquisite verses, made himself peculiarly the poet of Trinity. The chief event of his Cambridge life was, of course, his friendship for Arthur Henry Hallam, who lived, as is well known, in the New Court. Tennyson himself was otherwise not greatly attached to Cambridge. He lived at some distance from Trinity, in Corpus Buildings, and went down without taking his degree. In this respect, Thackeray (* Bogle), two years his junior, was very different from him. Through all his life, Thackeray, although he was so closely identified with London, kept his love for Cambridge, and was at heart a don. While still in residence, he would walk reading along one of the paths in the Great Court, and, in after life, he constantly returned. His rooms were close to Newton's, north of the Great Gate. Probably no one has handled University life with more success—the subject is proverbially difficult—than Thackeray in the early chapters of *Pendennis*; and, in most of his novels, he sent his heroes to colleges which, whether he placed them in Oxford or Cambridge, have all the features of his beloved Trinity.

With Thackeray we are hard on the heels of our own age. The modern period of Trinity's history begins with the mastership of William Whewell, whose name is inseparable from his college. The twenty-five years of his mastership, from 1841 to 1866, form a very distinguished epoch. As scholar, organiser, and benefactor to the foundation, he was pre-eminent. The famous epigram which said of him that "Science was his forte and omniscience his foible" was in the main true, but he carried to everything he attempted an immense interest and a sound judgment. His statue very worthily completes the group in the antechapel. It was erected during the mastership of his successor, William Hepworth Thompson (* Herkomer) the Platonist, famous for his erudition and his *bons mots*. Before his elevation to the mastership, Dr Thompson had been Regius Professor of Greek. The men of his generation who belonged to the Society were men of the highest eminence; the best known are, perhaps, Joseph Barber Lightfoot (* Richmond, Dickinson), the commentator on St Paul's Epistles and Bishop of Durham; James Clerk Maxwell,* Professor of Experimental Physics in the University; the late Arthur Cayley (* Dickinson), the greatest mathematician whom Trinity boasts since the days of Newton; and the Public Orator, W. G. Clark (bust by Woolner), Thompson's life-long friend. When Thompson died in 1886, he was succeeded by the present master, Dr Butler, who had been Head Master of Harrow and Dean of Gloucester. Beneath these rulers, and with the highest prestige in the world as her tradition, Trinity fully justifies her distinction as a royal foundation and a nursing-mother of sound and religious learning. To select from the present society is invidious; but the names of Professor Henry Sidgwick, Professor Michael Foster (* Herkomer), Dr Henry Jackson (* Furse), and Professor Jebb, are of European repute, to say nothing of the present vice-master, Mr Aldis Wright, editor of Shakspeare, and Mr John Willis Clark, the present Registrary, whose investigations in Cambridge history and antiquities are well known everywhere. In the Church one may point to the theologian Dr Westcott, Bishop of Durham, to Dr Farrar, Dean of Canterbury, and to the late Charles Alan Smythies, Bishop of Zanzibar; among politicians, to

Mr Arthur and Mr Gerald Balfour, and Sir William Harcourt; while of doctors, lawyers and men of letters the crowd cannot be numbered.

CHAPTER XVII

EMMANUEL COLLEGE

When one hears of the destruction of the beautiful courts at Emmanuel and Sidney, one is tempted to wonder what good genius of building spared the second court of St John's and Nevile's Court at Trinity. Had Ralph Symons' work been allowed to remain here, we should have had a building almost exactly parallel with the latter. Symons built courts, but he did not attempt imposing street-fronts, and the ranges he erected between 1584 and 1586 turned their backs ungraciously to the road. The entrance to the college was on the north side, where there is now a smaller court in the Gothic style of 1840. What is now known as the Brick Building, east of the entrance court and at right angles to the south side, belongs to 1633, but is substantially in harmony with Symons' earlier work. It forms a very charming fragment. The classical transformation of Emmanuel was begun during Dr Breton's mastership. Sir Christopher Wren, who was just completing his chapel at Pembroke, was invited to design the east side of the court. It is interesting to observe how he followed his uncle's design for the chapel of Peterhouse, copying the lateral galleries which connect the chapel with the main buildings. Wren built these between 1665 and 1677, and it is probable that, when he began working at Trinity in 1675, he left the completion of this beautiful composition to his pupil, Nicholas Hawksmoor. The characteristic of the whole is a very striking dignity. Internally, the chapel is less interesting, but the stained glass, representing noteworthy members of the college, such as Sancroft, William Law, and some of the Cambridge Platonists, is thoroughly suited to the fine, plain windows. The northern gallery is the picture-gallery of the Master's Lodge as well as an approach to the chapel, and contains a number of fine portraits, including a Lely, two Gainsboroughs and two Romneys.

In the last century the revival which Wren had innocently inaugurated swept away Symons' building. In 1719 the south side of the court was rebuilt; the gigantic pilasters in the centre are a proof of how bad the Palladian work of that overabused period could be. Sir James Burrough of Caius, who for half a century was the architectural dictator of Cambridge, designed new north and west buildings, obeying the unconquerable desire of the day for an eloquent façade. Because the design is Burrough's, this addition is tolerable and more or less appropriate to the chapel; but Burrough died before it was begun, and this, like the Clare chapel, is a posthumous and probably slanderous addition to his fame. At all events the work was entrusted to Essex, who carried it out before 1770. It is perhaps significant that Essex was chosen, a year or two later, to compare his work once more to Wren's, this time at Trinity. The western cloister, which recalls the similar but earlier building at Pembroke, is heavy but not unsuccessful. Essex had his own way with the Hall, which is probably the least agreeable hall in Cambridge. It is cold and stiff, and the plaster roof brings bad taste to a climax. In the Gothic court north of this is the Library, which corresponds to the refectory of the old Dominican house—the Hall is on the site of the chapel. It was, till the Restoration, the college chapel. Sancroft, to whose initiative Wren's work is due, gave it a valuable collection of old books, chiefly Bibles, and its Oriental manuscripts were carefully described by Sir William Jones. The chief modern addition to Emmanuel is the large brick building at the east end of the college garden. This, although not remarkable in itself, is interesting as the pioneer of an attempt to revive the economical principle of the medieval hostel. It also forms a not unfitting termination to the pretty lawn, with its pond and tennis-courts.

"The pure house of Emmanuel" occupies the site of the house of Dominican Friars outside Barnwell Gate. At the dissolution the buildings were left untouched, and, when Sir Walter Mildmay, Chancellor of the Exchequer and Treasurer of the Household, came into possession of the land, he had his materials for a college all ready. Sir Walter was a strong Puritan, and was on that account no great favourite with Queen Elizabeth. She met him one day and said, "Sir Walter, I hear that you have erected a Puritan foundation." Sir Walter, however, disclaimed the insinuation, "No, Madam; far be it from me to countenance anything contrary to your established laws; but I have set an acorn, which, when it becomes an oak, God alone knows what will be the fruit thereof." The acorn, nevertheless, grew into a very Puritan oak. The buildings seem to have been erected in a curious spirit; for, if not Sir Walter, at all events his executors, revelled in the fact that the secular buildings of the foundation stood upon the Friary church, and did all they could to obliterate the monastic plan of the buildings. But, beyond this unnecessary manifestation of spite, the college was admirably governed and its students were—and all through its history have been—serious and law-abiding. Sir Walter founded it as "a College of Theology, Science, Philosophy, and Literature, for the extension of the pure Gospel of Christ our only Mediator, to the honour and glory of Almighty God," and appointed, as its first master, Dr Laurence Chaderton, who ruled the college for thirty-eight years, and had a great part in the Authorised Version of the Bible. Under Dr Chaderton, the foundation increased in learning and godliness, and Fuller said of it, "Sure I am, at this day it hath overshadowed all the Universities, more than a moiety of the present masters of colleges being bred therein." Dr Branthwaite* of Caius, Dr Whichcot* of King's, Dr Samuel Ward* of Sidney, and the famous Ralph Cudworth* of Clare and Christ's, all held fellowships at Emmanuel.

As time went on, the Puritanism of Emmanuel became more and more pronounced. The services in the chapel savoured of Congregationalism and were altogether opposed to the Laudian revival of church life and doctrine. Under the first Dr Sancroft, the college ritual was thus reported to the Archbishop, "They receive that Holy Sacrament, sitting upon forms about the Communion Table, and do pull the Loaf one from the other, after the minister hath begun. And so the Cup, one drinking as it were to another, like good fellows, without any particular application of the said words, more than once for all." This expression of shocked piety has nothing in its wording which allows us to expect exaggeration. The servers at the altar were also "Fellows' subsizars," and not in holy orders. However, one fails to see any extravagant Protestantism in this arrangement. Emmanuel chapel must have presented a strange contrast to Wren's and Cosin's chapel at Peterhouse, or to the chapel at Queens' which Dowsing ransacked so unceremoniously. The college, meanwhile, was the nursery of American colonisers, and has therefore always been a goal of American pilgrimage. Mr Everett's bombastic passage on the subject has been often quoted; its eloquence is scarcely of the finest type. But, in company with a row of Pilgrim Fathers, Emmanuel produced John Harvard, the founder of the greatest American University, and may therefore be called the mother of American education.

But, in common with St John's and other colleges, Emmanuel lost its Puritanism with years. The Restoration brought in a better state of feeling, and, under the second Dr Sancroft and his successors, Doctors Breton* and Holbech,* the college devoted its energies to building. William Sancroft became Archbishop of Canterbury, and kept up the traditions of his college in refusing to acknowledge James II.'s Declaration. He was the chief of the seven bishops who signed the famous petition against that document. Afterwards, as a non-juror, he resigned his archbishoprick. But the best of all the sons of Emmanuel was another non-juror, William Law, who was for many years a fellow, and held the living of King's Cliffe in Northamptonshire. This great man has become better known to the world since the publication of his biography by Canon Overton, and the reprinting of his letters to Bishop Hoadly. He was a staunch and able supporter of the Church's principles, but his most abiding monument is the half mystical but intensely practical treatise called *A Serious Call to a Devout and Holy Life*. The book has had an influence second only to that of the *Pilgrim's Progress*, and its wide application may be judged from the fact that it affected people so widely different as Dr Johnson and Richard Hurrell Froude. Its simple but vivid style and its picturesque quaintness, account very largely for its popularity. In later years, Law, a solitary and meditative man, took up the half-understood ideas of German mysticism, and became a blind disciple of Jacob Behmen. These later aberrations have somewhat eclipsed his legitimate fame. The college has commemorated him by a window in the chapel. In connection with Law, it is interesting to remember that another mystical writer, Joseph Hall, Bishop, first of Exeter and afterwards of Norwich, was a fellow of Emmanuel. There is a portrait of Hall in the splendid collection at the Lodge, in which he is represented as wearing a gold medal. This medal was given him by the States General as a recognition of his services at the Synod of Dort, and the original is still in the possession of the college.

There is also, in the same collection, an admirable portrait of Sancroft, who, beyond his contributions to the new chapel, was a great benefactor to the library. This library is one of the most valuable in Cambridge. Bishop Bedell of Kilmore, who pursued his studies at Emmanuel with great success, and was a fellow of the college, left it a Hebrew Bible which he had bought for its weight in silver. Among other treasures it contains a MS. of Chrysostom and a copy of Wyclif's Bible, with the inscription "Ihū help us, for we ben feble." To return to the portraits in the Master's Lodge. We find there an excellent portrait of that accomplished diplomat and typical prig, Sir William Temple, by Lely. And, among other seventeenth-century worthies, we are glad to see the portrait of the greatest of Cambridge builders, Ralph Symons, "Effigies Radulphi Simons," the inscription goes, "Architecti sua aetate peritissimi qui praeter plurima aedificia ab eo praeclare facta, duo collegia Emanuelis hoc Sydneii illud exstruxit integre. Magnam etiam partem Trinitatis reconcinnavit amplissime."

After the time of Law and the non-jurors, the history of Emmanuel is very quiet, and the stately ease for which its buildings are conspicuous possessed the college. During the mastership of Dr William Richardson,* in 1765, a member of the college published a book which had a tremendous effect on English literature. This was the *Reliques of Ancient English Poetry*, collected by Bishop Percy of Dromore. The labours of this antiquarian are a lasting glory to his college. A similar taste was apparent in Richardson's successor, "rare" Richard Farmer (* Romney) who was master from 1775 to 1797. The love of himself and his *coterie* for Shakspeare took him, night after night, to the theatre at Stourbridge Fair, and his affection for the drama combined with his good-fellowship made him something of a curiosity at the time when most college masters were dry and pedantic. To the same period belongs Samuel Parr, whose pipe, tobacco-box, and stopper are preserved by the College. He was undoubtedly a wit and a good talker, but his jokes were lengthy and pompous, and he scarcely deserves the praise of those admirers who have likened him to Dr Johnson and Sydney Smith. For most of us, possibly, he lives entirely by virtue of de Quincey's essay upon him.

The two most famous scholars whom Emmanuel produced in the eighteenth century were Joshua Barnes,* Professor of Greek at its beginning, and Richard Hurd,* Bishop in succession of Lichfield and Worcester, who died in 1808. Hurd was a theologian with a somewhat dull pen, and is now chiefly remembered as the disciple, friend and biographer of Bishop Warburton. At the beginning of this century Sir Busick Harwood, a scientific man greatly in advance of his age, was Professor of Anatomy. Gell, the antiquary and explorer of Pompeii, who died in 1836, was also an Emmanuel man. But the present century, although the standard of work and scholarship has been high, is not prolific in eminent names. Our greatest living historian, Dr Creighton, held a fellowship at Emmanuel according to the terms of the Dixie Professorship, but Cambridge cannot count him as her own. At present, the college is rapidly increasing in numbers and emulates the modern popularity of Pembroke; and it has the distinction, rare at Cambridge, of success on the river and in the schools alike.

CHAPTER XVIII

SIDNEY SUSSEX COLLEGE

Ralph Symons, the great Cambridge builder whose name deserves to be more widely known than it is, was the architect chosen to superintend the works at Sidney. He was employed on Nevile's Court at Trinity, and was, a year or two later, to begin operations in the second court of St John's. Sidney, which was ready at the beginning of 1599, was quite comparable with those famous works of art. As usual, the architect did not attempt to manage a street-front. Here, however, instead of turning the back of his buildings to the street, as at Emmanuel, he constructed an oblong three-sided court, whose eastern side directly fronted the street. In 1628 Sir Francis Clerke of Houghton Conquest completed a second court on similar lines. The south side of one court thus became the north side of the other. This common side, which exactly bisects the building, was terminated by a gateway opening on the street and into either court. In this original plan the entrance to the Hall was immediately in the centre of the eastern range of the north court; the entrance to the Chapel occupied a similar position in the south court. We are still able to admire this graceful and simple plan. But of the original buildings the only remaining traces are the oriels in the garden-front of the Master's Lodge. In 1776 Essex, who had for the last ten years been "improving" Cambridge out of knowledge, built a new chapel; and in 1830, while Dr Chafy was master—the names of these masters deserve to be handed down—it was decided to thoroughly remodel the college in the new Gothic style. This step was prompted simply by the admiration which Wilkins' doings at Corpus, Trinity, and King's had excited. Each college glowed with pious emulation, and Sidney chose for its destroyer Sir Jeffrey Wyattville, who had Gothicised a great part of Windsor Castle. Wyattville overhauled the college in the Vandal manner; removed all traces, save those I have referred to, of Symons' obsolete work, and replaced it by the present pretentious and insipid structure which adorns the eastern side of Sidney Street. It is a comfort to know that a later generation has made amends for this criminal error of taste. A court, or rather two sides of a court, with cloisters, have been added in recent years by the late Mr John Loughborough Pearson. This range of buildings, not very obvious owing to the high walls behind which it stands, is of red brick, and, like many other new buildings in Cambridge, is in the style of the French Renaissance with English modifications. It is certainly one of Mr Pearson's great successes, and is, moreover, a success in a line which he seldom attempted. The court—which contains, by the way, a very fine Combination Room—is one of the most retired spots in Cambridge, and in its studious shades it is possible to forget Wyattville's ravages.

Sidney Sussex College

In 1589 died an excellent lady, Frances Lady Sussex, widow of the second Earl. She was the daughter of Sir William Sidney, and would in any case have achieved a negative distinction as the wife of Thomas Radcliffe and the aunt of Sir Philip Sidney. But in her will she left a legacy of five thousand pounds, to be employed by her executors in the foundation of a college at Cambridge, or, in case the bequest were insufficient, in enlarging Clare Hall. Six years later, the executors bought a site from Trinity College. When Henry VIII. founded Trinity, he made over to it the lands of the Franciscan Friary which, until the dissolution, had occupied the space between the modern Sidney Street and the King's Ditch. The buildings were apparently taken down and used as a quarry for Henry's new college. Thus the site was vacant, and the executors, after making a preliminary payment of a hundred marks, took over the ground on a perpetual lease, and engaged to pay a rent of £13. 6s. 8d. yearly. These executors, the actual founders of Sidney, were the Earl of Kent and Sir John Harrington, the translator of Ariosto. The college was called the College of the Lady Frances Sidney Sussex, and took her arms, Radcliffe impaling Sidney. The pheon, the heraldic symbol of the Sidneys, is the badge of the college, and, like the eagle of St John's and the silver crescent of Trinity Hall, has given its title to the college magazine of our own days.

The first master was appointed in 1598. He was Dr James Montagu,* and became Bishop of Winchester, where he died in 1618. But, in spite of this augury, the history of Sidney is the reverse of prelatical. Of late years, the college has somewhat retrieved its past record, but, on the whole, its distinction is Puritan. It is, however, a college whose history finds its centre in one event, and that event is vague and shadowy. In the college books, under the date April 23rd, 1616, is the following inscription, "Oliverus Cromwell, Huntingdoniensis, admissus ad commensum sociorum Aprilis vicesimo sexto; Tutore Mag° Ricardo Howlet." Few colleges boast such a fellow-commoner. The note which follows, written in after years by a good Royalist, is worth transcribing: "Hic fuit grandis ille impostor, carnifex perditissimus, qui, pientissimo rege Carolo primo nefaria caede sublato, ipsum usurpavit thronum, et tria regna per quinque ferme annorum spatium, sub protectoris nomine, indomita tyrannide vexavit." Vexavit, as Polonius would say, is good. No language is more abusive than aptly handled Latin! This "big impostor and most damn'd butcher" stayed at Cambridge till July, 1617, and then, like many great men, left without taking his degree. His contribution to the social life of his college has been stigmatised as discreditable, but this is probably invidious rumour and nothing more. The window of his room—which, by the way, dates from 1827 or thereabout—is still shown to the credulous. There is an admirable portrait of him in the hall, which was presented to the college, with a rather unnecessary parade of anonymity, by Mr Holles of the Hyde in Essex.

The great name of Cromwell must not, however, suffer us to forget the names of the good and pious men whom Sidney has nurtured. Dr Edmund Calamy, the famous Nonconformist divine, was a member of the college. So was Thomas Wilson, Bishop of Sodor and Man. So, too, were Jones of Nayland, the revivalist and hymn-writer, and an even more famous Evangelical preacher, Thomas Cecil. Sidney had, indeed, a very conspicuous share in the revival of spiritual life at the end of the last century. On the other hand, the college produced, by way of an anomaly, Sir Roger l'Estrange, the Royalist pamphleteer, whose sympathies were certainly apart from his education. The laborious antiquary, Thomas Rymer of the *Fœdera,* was also a Sidney man. In our own century it has been recorded that—

> There was a young man of Sid. Sussex
> Who stated that w + x
> Was the same as xw!
> So they said, "We will trouble you
> To confine those ideas to Sid. Sussex."

But any such misconception has been rectified by the present master, Mr Charles Smith, whose mathematical text-books are classics in their own branch of literature. And, among living members of the college, we may notice the present Bishop of Bloemfontein, Dr John Wale Hicks, who is not only celebrated for his equal skill in medicine and divinity, but, as tutor of his college and vicar of Little St Mary's, has had perhaps the greatest spiritual influence on modern Cambridge life. Although Sidney is a small college, there is none which is so remarkable for the patriotism and good-fellowship existing among its undergraduates; and, within very recent years, it has supplied the University with excellent athletes, and one of its members has become president of the Union.

CHAPTER XIX

DOWNING COLLEGE

James Wilkins, the builder of Downing, must be distinguished from the later William Wilkins, the gothic experimentalist. If the second Wilkins had worked in the manner of the first, we should have missed some valuable historical relics, but should have gained in other respects. Downing, with its heavy angularities and immense porticoes, is not a very great advance on the plans so cherished by Mr James Essex, but it bears the marks of a good intention, and is an excellently proportioned building. It was begun in 1807, but has never been finished, and now simply consists of two parallel ranges running north and south, with a wide space of lawn between them. Its situation is very remote, but to this it owes its chief beauty, the lovely park with its fine avenues. The view northwards from the park, embracing the fellows' garden, and ending in the towers of the new Roman Catholic Church, is worth seeing, although the contrast of the classical college with one of the latest examples of modern Gothic work is somewhat inharmonious.

Downing is almost the youngest of Cambridge colleges, and its history is chiefly concerned with its foundation. At Gamlingay, in the only part of Cambridgeshire that can be called picturesque, there lived from about 1680 to 1749, a baronet named Sir George Downing. He had been the victim of a compulsory marriage. At the early age of fifteen, he had been married to his cousin Mary Forester, who herself was only thirteen. They never lived together, and in 1717, Sir George made a will by which he bequeathed his estates to some collateral relatives. This document contained the provision that, if his heirs died out, the estates were to be applied to the use of a college which his trustees should found in Cambridge. He nevertheless outlived the trustees, and, dying in 1749, left his property to his collateral heir, Sir Jacob Downing. Sir Jacob was married, but died without issue in 1764. His wife retained the estates, but this gave rise to a long lawsuit, and, at her death, Chancery pronounced the original will to be valid. The Charter was granted in 1800, but the buildings were not begun till 1807, and the college was not in working order till 1821.

Sir George Downing's design had included a master and sixteen fellows. In addition—presumably to confer some prestige upon a late foundation—he had provided for two professorships in connection with the college, the Downing Professorships of Medicine and of the Laws of England. Although the influx of undergraduates was at first very small, the valuable law scholarships attracted many students in course of time. The second master, Mr Serjeant Frere,* was an eminent lawyer, and is still renowned as the first of college masters who dispensed their hospitality without too keen an eye to rigid selection. Dr Annesley, the first master, from 1805 to 1812, was the head of a college which had no corporate existence, and Mr Frere, for nine years, was in a similar position. Downing has the misfortune of being in a very remote, although charming situation, and the number of her undergraduates has never been very large. But her present society includes the Professor of Law, Dr Maitland; and her master, Dr Alexander Hill, is a distinguished ornament of the medical school. And, among the doctors who have been educated at Downing are the late Sir George Humphrey, Professor Latham, and one of the best known of living physicians, Professor Bradbury.

CHAPTER XX

SELWYN COLLEGE, ETC.

The memory of George Augustus Selwyn, the great Bishop, first of Melanesia, afterwards of Lichfield, is honoured in Cambridge by the latest of all the colleges. Selwyn, one of a famous Cambridge family, died in 1877; and in 1882, Selwyn College was opened. The object of the college is that which had, some time before, prompted the foundation of Keble—the provision of University education at a more moderate rate than had hitherto been the case. It is conducted on what is known as the hostel system; that is to say, its members, while enjoying all University privileges, have all their meals in common, and are supplied with most necessaries at fixed rates from the college buttery. This is, we may believe, the simple system out of which great foundations like Trinity grew; and, since Selwyn began it, one or two other colleges have pursued it with some success on a voluntary principle. At Selwyn, however, the hostel life is compulsory; and the college is known officially as Selwyn Hostel. It has not lived long enough to produce any great sons as yet, but its record is honourable, and we may expect much from it in the future.[8] Its buildings, forming two sides of a quadrangle, are of red brick, and were designed by Sir Arthur Blomfield, who also built the Master's Lodge at the east corner of the enclosure. As the essence of the college's existence is to provide accommodation for students, the buildings are devoted to rooms, and the Hall and Chapel were left to the last. For the first thirteen years of the history of the college, these necessities of college life were supplied by the low range of temporary buildings just inside the entrance gate. There, too, for some time to come the Hall will have to remain, a very simple room, whose only ornament is the portrait of Mr Arthur Lyttelton, late master and now vicar of Eccles. This, by Mr C. W. Furse, is a striking example of the New English school. In 1895, however, one of the wishes of the college was fulfilled, and the present noble Chapel was erected from Sir Arthur Blomfield's design. It stands north of the Master's Lodge, and is a very large and lofty building of red brick, with freestone dressings. The style is a free adaptation of English Perpendicular, the admirable window tracery being a remarkable feature. The interior is very good, and the very complete set of stalls, with their grotesque carvings and modern misereres, would do honour to a medieval collegiate church. Its consecration by the Bishop of Ely in October, 1895, was one of the most imposing ceremonies which have been seen of late years in Cambridge. The late Archbishop of Canterbury and several other prelates assisted at the function, and the sermon at mid-day was preached by the Archbishop. If the pious founders of

[8] Professor W. E. Collins, of King's College, London, the historian, should, however, be mentioned as an undergraduate and late tutor of Selwyn.

the older colleges had been able to be present, and had seen the whole college walk in procession round the quadrangle in the early morning, singing the sixty-eighth psalm, and had assisted at the celebration of the Holy Eucharist which followed, they would assuredly have thanked God that the traditions of their Church and of the University which was its daughter were preserved and cherished by more modern foundations.

Ridley Hall represents a school of thought somewhat different from that to which Selwyn owes its being, and is altogether a modern development in University life. Like Selwyn, it has an Oxford counterpart in Wycliffe Hall. It was founded in 1879 as a training college for those who, having already graduated from some college, wish to proceed to Holy Orders. Under the headship of Doctor Moule, it has already sent out several distinguished members of the Evangelical party, and has also been of great service to missionary societies. It has certainly proved itself a power in modern Cambridge, chiefly through the influence of its eminent principal; and has encouraged other religious bodies to attempt what is an accomplished fact in Oxford. The Presbyterian body are now building themselves a large theological college at the corner of the Madingley Road. The buildings of Ridley are not unlike those of Selwyn, and the Renaissance chapel with its picturesque iron turret is a pleasing object from most points of view. The architect of the older portion was Mr Charles Luck; the chapel and southern range were designed by Mr W. Wallace.

After many vicissitudes, Ayerst Hall has at length disappeared. Some years ago the Rev. W. Ayerst of Caius College established a small college on the hostel principle, which occupied the buildings now known as Queen Anne's Terrace, between Parker's Piece and the University Cricket Ground. In 1894 his students vacated these buildings for a new range between the Huntingdon and Madingley Roads, and their original home is now the offices of the University Correspondence College. Rather less than three years later, the venture was abandoned, and the new buildings were purchased for a colony of Benedictines. Since the building of the great church of Our Lady of the Assumption and the English Martyrs, which is so conspicuous a feature from the railway, the influx of Roman Catholic students has been much greater. In 1896 a Roman Catholic chaplaincy was founded in both Universities. The direct result of this measure was the purchase of Ayerst Hall and the establishment of a theological school for Roman Catholic undergraduates. This scheme is in its infancy, and its future remains to be seen. The new hostel is known as Edmund House.

Another abortive attempt was Cavendish College, founded in 1882, which took its name and coat-of-arms from the late Duke of Devonshire. By an irony of fate, it is the only collegiate building which the passer-by sees from the train—that is, unless he keeps a sharp lookout for King's Chapel. It was, however, a mile from the nearest college, on the furthest outskirts of the town, and, after a precarious existence, it failed and was closed in 1891. Between 1891 and 1895 the curious might roam through its halls unchecked, inspect the deserted library and the singularly comfortable buildings, and muse on the names of departed occupants inscribed on the staircases. Some of its students went down; others joined other colleges. In 1895 it was bought by Mr J. C. Horobin of Homerton, who transferred to it his training-college for schoolmasters and schoolmistresses. Its part in University life is not over yet, but its proud title has been exchanged for the more suburban name of Homerton, and now only old-fashioned people call it Cavendish.

Lastly, there is Fitzwilliam Hall. The same desire which led to the foundation of Selwyn and Keble led to the passing of a grace by the Senate of both Universities, by which students were allowed to become members of the University without joining any particular college. Unattached students now form a considerable element at both Oxford and Cambridge. The necessity for a certain amount of combination goes, nevertheless, without saying; and its result is Fitzwilliam Hall. A house opposite the Fitzwilliam Museum has been purchased, and has been turned into a club for non-collegiate students. There are a reading-room, lecture rooms, and rooms for the tutors, who are, for the most part, distinguished members of the older foundations. The non-collegiates have their own gown, their boat on the river, and their own clubs and societies; and, although some of their most promising members in time join other colleges, they have a distinct corporate life and status of their own. Thus, although Cambridge has in none of these respects been in front of her traditionally conservative sister, she has at all events followed not very far behind her in any.

CHAPTER XXI

GIRTON AND NEWNHAM

A few words must be devoted to these foundations, which, it cannot be doubted, are destined to play so important a part in the future life of the University. In the last chapter, I said that some of the founders would have rejoiced to see a ceremony so much in keeping with traditional usage as the consecration of Selwyn Chapel. It is at least doubtful whether Henry VI. would have looked with approval on the lady students who are so assiduous worshippers at his chapel; and even his imperious consort, the foundress of Queens', and the Lady Margaret herself, with her rooms in Christ's, would have probably hesitated to admit their own sex to the privileges of University life. But "the old order changeth," and colleges for women are not only accomplished facts, but facts which are very lively indeed. Till within the last half century, the University's estimate of the rights of women was very oriental: unmarried fellows were the rule, and masters' wives formed a very distinct social clique. But the breaking-down of these barriers came in time, and, with the ensuing civilisation, came the project for giving women the privileges of University education. "You know what women's minds are," wrote Erasmus scornfully of his patroness to a friend. The Professors who to-day occupy Erasmus' numerous chairs have plenty of opportunity of seeing that women's minds are not to be dismissed in a phrase. At any rate, woman has stormed Cambridge, and made a considerable breach in the fortifications, and the most doctrinaire of conservatives cannot keep her from the closely guarded citadel of the degree.

Girton is the earlier of the two colleges. It was started at Hitchin in 1869, and was removed to Cambridge in 1873. Even then it planted itself outside the hallowed precinct, on the brow of a hill, beside the straightest of all straight roads. Every Girton student knows, to her cost, the long avenue of telegraph posts which separates her from Cambridge; and although this approach, in fine weather, provides excellent landscapes in Hobbéma's best manner, in wet weather it is exceptionally dismal. She has her compensation, however, in the beautiful view which her college commands; and the buildings, although externally of rather various merit, are inside as comfortable as any in modern Cambridge. The style of the building is a mixed Gothic, and the older parts have a very mellow, aged look, but the entrance tower and its wings are built of a singularly disagreeable brick, which, one may hope, will in time be concealed by ivy or some other creeper. The college takes its name from the village of Girton, about half a mile to the north. The church of Girton is worth seeing.

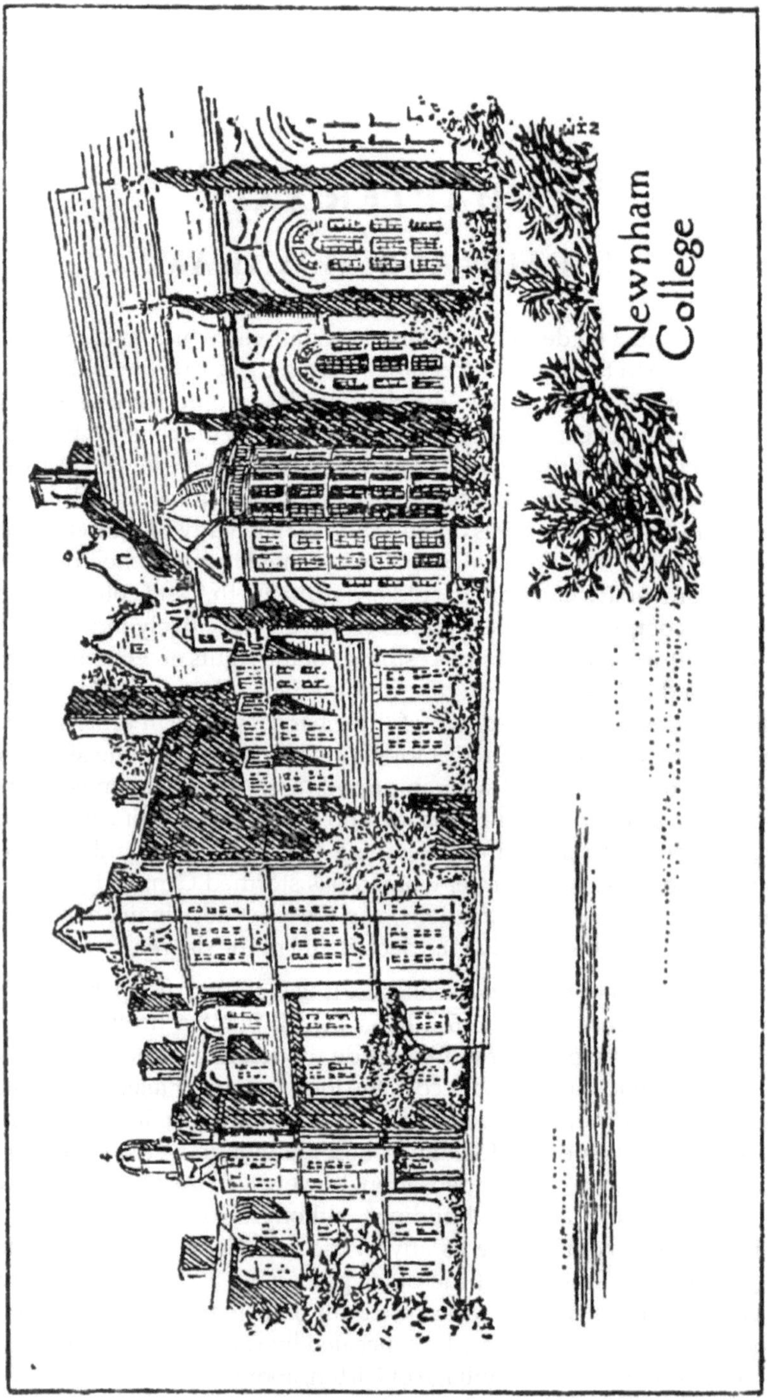

Newnham College

Newnham, which is in Cambridge itself, is a later foundation, but its progress has been astonishing. It also takes its name from a suburban village which has gradually become part of the town. The buildings of Newnham form a very imposing array, and are a remarkable contrast, with their Renaissance gables, to the Gothic buildings of Selwyn, just across the road. Mr Basil Champneys has produced in them one of the best modern imitations of French Renaissance; and their outline, seen at a favourable distance, would not be unworthy of Chambord or Chenonceaux. The oldest part is the Old Hall, forming the south-eastern angle of the college; this belongs to 1875. Then came Clough Hall on the north side. Sidgwick Hall followed it, and completed this side, and, in 1894, two sides of a quadrangle were finished and the Old Hall joined to the rest by the erection of the Pfeiffer Building. In this latest part of the college is the principal gateway, now closed by a double gate of beautiful ironwork, in memory of the first principal, Miss Clough. In the hall are portraits of Miss Clough, Professor and Mrs Sidgwick, and Miss M. G. Kennedy, by Mr J. J. Shannon, and one (by Richmond) of Miss Helen Gladstone, who till lately was one of the leading Newnham dons. Young as they are, both Girton and Newnham have their history, and are able to inspire their students with a patriotism which is the natural result of extraordinary perseverance and hardly-won victories.

CHAPTER XXII

THE UNIVERSITY BUILDINGS

Fond tradition would compel us to accept the so-called School of Pythagoras as the *fons et origo* of the medieval University. However, the legend does not go for very much, and we may suppose that, until the foundation of several colleges brought about the necessity of a common centre, education was carried on in the numerous monastic houses or by private teachers at their own lodgings. The present schools, within the limits of the University Library, are probably in part of the fourteenth century, but, for the most part, belong to the latter half of the next century. They are not very conspicuous, and probably ninety-nine out of a hundred Cambridge men have never been inside them, as the majority of public examinations are held in the Senate House and the various large halls of which the town is full. They are, moreover, so incorporated in the Library as to form part of the building, and have no very distinctive mark.

The architectural history of the Library is singularly complex. It occupies two quadrangles north of and running parallel with King's Chapel. The first of these is the quadrangle of the schools, and is entered from the open space between the Senate House and King's; the second occupies the site of the original quadrangle of King's, and is entered from the opposite side. Mr G. G. Scott has restored the old gateway with some success, and it forms a good contrast to the opposite gateway at Clare. Round these courts are grouped the very various Library buildings. The Library itself is entered from the eastern side, to which it presents a very stiff classical front. Somewhere between 1470 and 1480, the great prelate, Thomas Rotherham, then fellow of King's and Bishop of Lincoln, built a Perpendicular façade on this side; and this was the beginning of the buildings. Hitherto the few books which the Library contained, mostly bequeathed by Dr Richard Holme in 1424, had been placed in the present south gallery on the first floor of the quadrangle. The opposite gallery was then the Senate House. The western gallery, above the school of Canon Law, overlooked the Court of King's. Rotherham thus completed the first quadrangle, and, until the eighteenth century, the Library was contained in the eastern, southern and western rooms. Mr Clark, in his picturesque notes on Cambridge, assures us that it must have been hopelessly neglected. The days of building prelates were long past when, in 1715, George I., for some unknown reason, purchased the library of Dr John Moore, Bishop in succession of Norwich and Ely, and presented it to the University. Just about the same time, he had sent a regiment to enforce loyalty on Oxford. The epigrams which passed between the Tory and Whig Universities on this occasion have been so often quoted as to need no repetition. The Oxford epigram takes the palm for neatness, but the Cambridge retort was the last word on the subject.

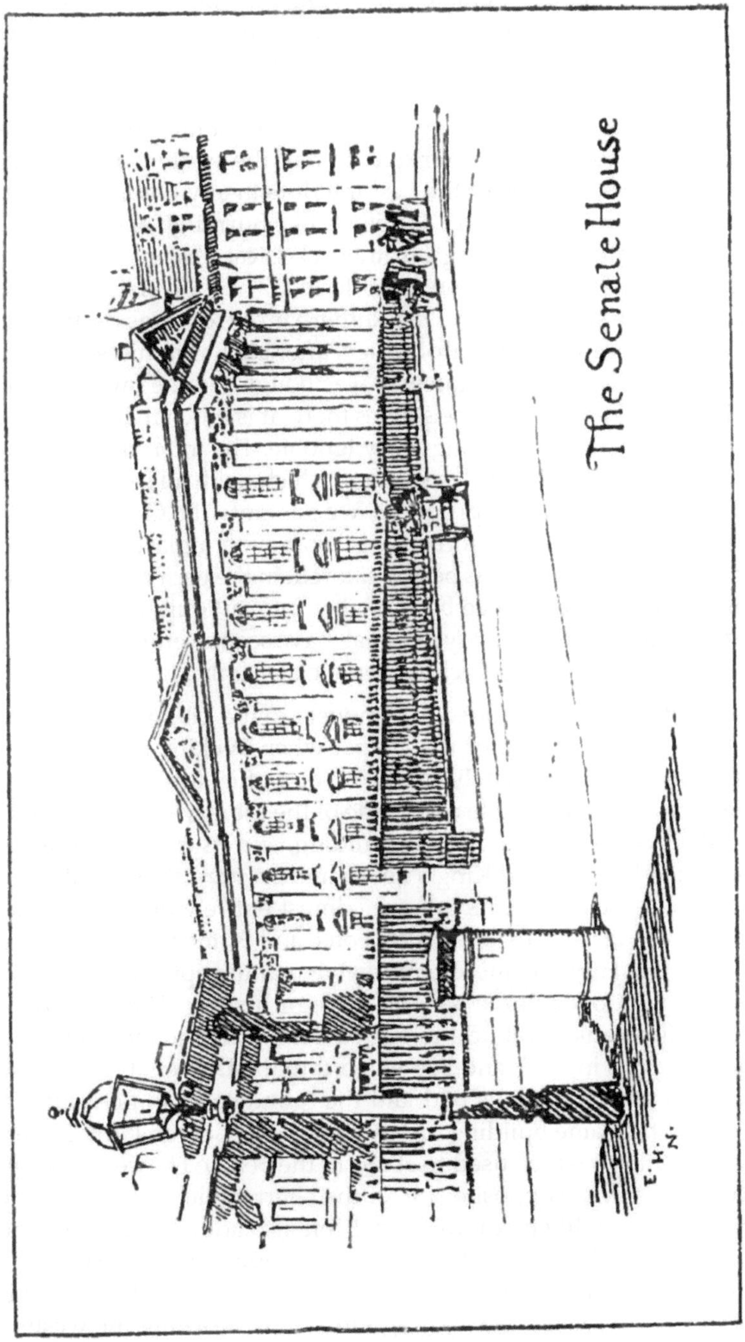

The Senate House

However, although King George's gift cannot be valued too highly as a benefaction to Cambridge, and was also an incentive to wit of a very felicitous order, it was in one way rather unfortunate. The books were many; accommodation was small. It was proposed to place the addition in what was then the Senate House, and to build a new meeting-place for the University. Mr Burrough of Caius submitted a plan for the new Senate House, of which we can see the result to-day. The quadrangle was thus entirely given over to the Library. It must have formed one of the most beautiful in Cambridge; to-day the western room, running between the two courts, has one of the best interiors in any library. But the age was hostile to medieval buildings. With architects like Burrough and Gibbs—excellent architects, both of them—carrying out their classical designs on either side, the Library was not suffered to remain unmolested. The University decided to harmonise it with these structures. In 1754 Rotherham's front was destroyed, and the present Georgian façade was put up, which, after all, harmonises very badly with the Senate House. Rotherham's gateway was bought by the owner of Madingley Hall, and is now the entrance to the stables there. It is much to be regretted, for the present aspect of the Library is singularly ignoble. The interior, however, offers a better contrast. From the classical east room, which, with all its plastered ugliness, is certainly stately and not inappropriate, we pass into the Catalogue Room, once the Senate House. Somebody adorned this room with a plaster ceiling in the last century, but the old timber roof is being restored. In the west room, which contains some valuable woodwork, we go back further into antiquity, and, when we have completed the circuit of the Library, we shall have seen a series of buildings which, in their diversity, are thoroughly characteristic of Cambridge.

The present century has added enormously to the Library. King's transferred itself finally to the other side of the chapel when Wilkins finished his range of buildings—that is, approximately in 1830. Soon after this the important *annexe* which now constitutes the whole north side of the Library was added. Its architect was Mr C. R. Cockerell. It is a colossal building, and its external ugliness may be fully appreciated from the old King's quadrangle, where all the buildings in front of it have been cleared away. Its interior, almost entirely devoted to theology, is as fine and imposing as its exterior is hideous, and is, moreover, a very agreeable room for students. Here the more remarkable manuscripts are exhibited, among which the famous Codex Bezae has the place of honour. Theodore Béza, whose name is in the first rank of Biblical critics, saved it from the sack of the monastery of St Irénée at Lyons in 1562, and presented it to the University—a gift worthy of the academy in which Erasmus had laid the foundations of Scriptural study. At the west end of the same building are the statues of George I. (by Rysbrack) and George II. (by Wilton) which used to stand in the Senate House. Cockerell's work finds its antithesis in the opposite side of the court, which was rebuilt by Sir Gilbert Scott on a thoroughly medieval plan. Scott also added a second storey to this side, which, like Cockerell's building, was continued into the eastern court. He also entirely refaced the front opposite King's Chapel. The effect is uniform, but gloomy. His son completed the existing Library by restoring the western façade. The rooms on the ground floor are also appropriated to books, principally modern and lighter literature, but contain nothing worth seeing. Cockerell's building is an exception, for its ground floor is occupied by the Woodwardian Museum of Geology.

In spite of the misfortunes which it brought about, the Senate House is one of those buildings which gave Cambridge its greatest dignity. One may hesitate to compare it with the Radcliffe Library at Oxford, which was finished about twenty-five years later, but it is largely due to the same architect and is certainly an addition to his credit. Gibbs had, however, only a small share in the work, for Burrough is its real designer. It is an oblong building, with entrances on the east and on the middle of the south sides. It has a double range of windows throughout, save on the west side, where they are blank. Those in the upper storey are round-headed, those in the lower are square-headed and are surmounted by plain architraves, alternately round and pointed. The whole building is surrounded by an order of composite pilasters, cut square save near the doors, where they are round and fluted. Above the cornice is a balustrade, broken judiciously by the pediments of the entrances, which give the building its distinctive feature. The whole is one of the best specimens of early Georgian architecture in England, and the interior is perfectly consonant with the simple grandeur of the outside. The oak galleries suit the building admirably. At the east end, near the door, are the statues of the Duke of Somerset, Chancellor at the Revolution, and of William Pitt: the first by Rysbrack, the second by Nollekens.

After the Senate House, geographically and in point of time, comes the Pitt Press in Trumpington Street, a very glorious achievement of the early Gothic revivalists. Mr Bowes' list, published a year or two ago, is the monumental record of Cambridge printing, but, when the Pitt Press was founded, the traditions of John Siborch, who had set up a press in the University about 1521, had been almost forgotten. Even since then, the Pitt Press, although the parent of Professor Jebb's edition of Sophocles and other masterpieces of erudition, has scarcely proved itself the rival of the Clarendon. Its origin is curious. After the Great Commoner's death, a subscription fund was started to commemorate him, the immediate results of which were the statues in Westminster Abbey and Hanover Square. The rest of the money was employed in building the Pitt Press. In the chronological order of works of the date, it stands just after Wilkins' screen at King's, and just before Rickman's court at St John's. Its architect was Edward Blore, and it was finished in 1833. It is not uglier than most buildings of the period, and the gateway tower looks well at a sufficient distance. This tower, by the way, has often given rise to the impression that it is an ecclesiastical building of some kind, and it is known generally as the "freshman's church." The hoax used at one time to be practised on unsuspecting young gentlemen during their early days of residence, but the epithet is now too well known to be misleading.

Further on, and on the same side of Trumpington Street, is the Fitzwilliam Museum. In 1816 died Richard, Viscount Fitzwilliam, who bequeathed his library and pictures to the University. He left also £100,000 for the building of a museum to receive them. His princely benefaction was, of course, accepted; and, pending the erection of a building, the collections were deposited in the old Perse School, now the Engineering Laboratory. Building was not begun till late in the thirties, when Basevi was employed to execute the present design. Basevi, however, fell from the great tower of Ely before the work was finished, and what he had begun was continued by Mr Cockerell. This architect had earned a dubiously just reputation for his proceedings at the University Library; here he had an excellent plan to work on, and did justice to it. The Fitzwilliam Museum, with the exception of certain decorations, was completed in 1847; the collections, augmented meanwhile by private bequests, were brought from the Perse School in 1848. Differences of opinion exist as to the merit of the building and the collections, but there can be no doubt that the façade is, after that of St Paul's, one of the best of its kind anywhere. It is astonishingly good for its period. The decoration of the entrance hall is splendid but meretricious, and the lavish profusion of coloured marbles is almost suspicious. A statue of the Prince Consort is the cynosure of this brilliancy, and there is a portrait of him in the basement, dressed in his Chancellor's robes, with a red curtain and the great gate of Trinity in the background. For the most part the basement is devoted to the University Museum of Antiquities, the nucleus of which was bequeathed by Samuel Disney of the Hyde, Essex. In memory of this gentleman has been founded the Disney Professorship of Archæology. On the ground-floor also is the valuable Fitzwilliam Library, and a very perfect library of musical works. In one of the rooms part of the valuable collection of engravings is exhibited. This comprises specimens of early Flemish and German artists, Albert Dürer, the Little Masters of Germany, and most of the best workers in wood-cut, steel-engraving, and mezzotint. Others may be found upstairs among the pictures. The pictures are of various merit, and many are copies. The fine Paul Veronese, "Mercury turning Aglauros into stone," which faces the principal door of the west gallery, is undoubtedly genuine, and there are some good examples of the Venetian school, especially two small pictures attributed to Palma the younger. Lovers of early Italian art will find a small Madonna and Child by Pinturicchio, while the disciples of the now unpopular Bolognese school will admire the picture of St Roch and the Angel, by Annibale Caracci. The room also contains a doubtful Rembrandt, two exquisitely finished little pictures by Gerard Douw, some good Ruysdaels, a Teniers or two, and a picture which, legend says, is the earliest Murillo in existence. There are also portraits by Gainsborough and Hogarth.

The south room is even more miscellaneous. It is presided over by a vast copy of a Veronese, probably by the artist's brother, opposite which, on either side of the entrance from the main gallery, are two portraits of the school of Holbein, one of a bygone Fitzwilliam. The other was given by the executors of the late Dean of Lincoln, and represents a person unknown. Besides these, there are numerous small pictures of the late Italian type, and views of Venice by Canaletto and Zuccarelli. A very admirable Raeburn will appeal to all lovers of portrait art, and deserves wider fame. But the gem of the whole collection, a series of water-colours by Turner, is in this room. Mr Ruskin generously presented the University with these, and they may be reckoned among its most priceless treasures. In the eastern continuation of the room is the collection of small pictures given by Mr Daniel Mesman in 1834. Some of these, including a small landscape attributed to Ruysdael and some delicate pictures by Adam Elzheimer, are of considerable value; but the rest are somewhat devoid of interest. On the south wall is a set of small pictures of the

French school, mostly by Boucher, but two are attributed to Watteau, and two to Greuze. They are, however, of no great worth. And the rooms on the opposite side of the building are very uninteresting. Sir John Millais' famous "Bridesmaid" is in the western room of the two, in company with some English landscapes, Mr Watts' portrait of the late Duke of Devonshire, and Mr Richmond's portrait of the present Bishop of Durham. The eastern room is occupied by an immense model of the Taj Mehál, and by some very early Italian pictures, the most prominent of which is by Cosimo Rosselli, the painter whose startling use of colour was so acceptable to Pope Sixtus IV. Under the curatorship of Professor Colvin and the late Professor Middleton, the interest of the Museum was much increased; and the present curator, Dr James, the well-known theologian and antiquarian, has followed in their footsteps.

Since the days of Lord Fitzwilliam's bequest, the University's ardour has been turned in the direction of science. Most of the public buildings since then, such as the huge laboratories and Anatomical Museum (a work of Salvin's) are devoted to that interest, and the visitor will find them more utilitarian than anything else. In speaking of Pembroke, I have already referred to Mr Scott's façade to the Chemical Laboratory. The archæologist, however, will be greatly relieved to find the beautiful timber roof of the Perse school still existing where he least expects it—namely, in the Engineering Laboratory. These buildings, however, and others, such as the Observatory in the Madingley Road, and Sir Digby Wyatt's extraordinary façade at Addenbrooke's Hospital, which, the famous "Cambridge Freshman" was gravely informed, was the Vice-Chancellor's official residence, speak for themselves. Not the least important feature of modern Cambridge is the unobtrusive red-brick building in Mill Lane, occupied by the University Extension Syndicate. Not remarkable in itself, it is the visible sign of the aim of the modern University not to keep its cherished learning to itself, but to distribute its advantages to others. Whether or no the idea expressed by a far-sighted don in the last century, when he said that each town ought to have its university, will be realised, is a possibility that rests on the knees of the gods; but the means are certainly in use, and the wish is in a fair way of fulfilment.

CHAPTER XXIII

THE CHURCHES OF CAMBRIDGE

Although the architectural interest of Cambridge, so far as churches are concerned, is centred in the college chapels, there are nevertheless several churches which are not devoid of interest, and one or two which are quite unique. The visitor who takes the trouble to examine them will be amply repaid, although his reminiscences of them will, after a cursory inspection, be rather confused. Starting, then, from the western door of the University Church, and proceeding along King's Parade, he will find, just opposite King's gateway, the narrow passage which leads to St Edward's Church. St Edward's occupies the centre of a flagged court, and its east end faces Peas Hill, one of those Cambridge hills whose slope is invisible. It is a fairly large church with broad aisles and a short tower at the west end, and is mostly of the Decorated period, from 1340 to 1350; but it has been from time to time restored, and the tower suffers from a hideous coating of stucco. The nave arcade is lofty but rather meagre. The font is interesting, and was restored by the Cambridge Camden Society in the first half of the century. There are also good Decorated sedilia in the chancel. It was one of the centres of reforming influence in Cambridge, and many of the Marian martyrs, including Latimer, preached in it.

The next turning on the same side of King's Parade is Bene't Street, in which, at the corner of Free School Lane, is the very interesting church of St Benedict, long the chapel of Corpus Christi College. Although the nave and chancel of this church were thoroughly restored in 1869 and are very normal examples of later Gothic work, the tower and western arch belong to a very early period, certainly anterior to the Norman Conquest. The tower is rather thicker than most towers of its date, and rises to a very respectable height, but it has the characteristic trait of growing thinner as it reaches the top. The window-openings of the upper storey are small and primitive; that in the centre of each face is double, its two lights being separated by a small baluster-shaped column, as is the case at Earl's Barton in Northamptonshire and at other places. The tower-arch, inside the church, is very curious. It is tall and narrow, and is also thinner as it reaches the top; the pilasters which support it on either side have roughly carved capitals. One may safely refer the whole structure to the reign of Edward the Confessor, and possibly earlier. There are two somewhat similar towers at Lincoln, and a ruder, but later, tower at Oxford. A staircase still connects the south-west corner of the chancel with the old court of Corpus.

On the other side of Corpus is the church of St Botolph, a picturesque building, chiefly of Perpendicular date, which belonged for three centuries to the priory at Barnwell. Like most churches in Cambridge, it counted the undergraduates of one or two of the medieval colleges among its congregation, and the advowson now belongs to Queens' College. It is a fine, spacious church, and its plain tower, with the strange crawling beasts which serve as waterspouts, is one of the very various objects which contribute to the academical perspective of Trumpington Street. There is a good modern window by Mr C. E. Kempe at the east end of the north aisle.

Not very far on, just opposite Pembroke, is the extremely beautiful church of St Mary—known as Little St Mary's to distinguish it from the University Church. It is the most venerable object in a very heterogeneous group of buildings. Dwarfing it on one side is Burrough's classical wing at Peterhouse, and, on the other, is the tower of the new Congregational Chapel, a creditable imitation of the Belfry at Tournai. These, however, show it to advantage, and add to its venerable aspect. It is a very lovely example of the later Decorated style, and was built in 1352 on the site of the old church of St Peter. There is a tradition that Alan de Walsingham, who designed the Octagon at Ely, had something to do with it, and the very elaborate tracery of the east window is certainly worthy of a master's hand. It was for two hundred and eighty years the chapel of Peterhouse, and, as at St Bene't's, the passage from college to church is still preserved. Its shape is that of a college chapel; there are no side-aisles; and, save in the two bays south of the sanctuary, the church is lighted by a series of very large windows. There are two good brasses, one of a doctor of medicine in his robes, the other of a lady. It was restored by Sir Gilbert Scott, and, since then, a western choir-vestry has been added. In 1891, the east window was thoroughly restored and glass thoroughly worthy of it was added by the munificence of Mr Hamblin Smith. This window, a conventional treatment of the Annunciation, may be regarded as the best of Mr Kempe's many excellent windows. The small west window was also filled by Mr Kempe in 1894, but in this he has been less successful. It is to be hoped that the rest of the windows will be similarly treated.

Little St Mary's is almost at the extremity of Cambridge, and is the last church on the Trumpington Road. On the Hills Road, which may be reached by turning to the left just opposite the Leys School, are the not very beautiful St Paul's Church, which is a district church in the large parish of St Andrew the Less, and the great Roman Catholic church. This fine modern building, by Messrs Hansom of Newcastle, was built at the expense of Mrs Lyne Stevens, and was consecrated in 1890. The glass, by Powell of Whitefriars, is interesting but might be better. There is no church between this and Christ's College, opposite which is St Andrew's the Great, rebuilt in 1843, and remarkable for nothing save a memorial tablet in the chancel to Captain Cook the navigator. Holy Trinity, at the next street-corner, is in the main a Perpendicular church, but has been much added to in the present century. Charles Simeon was for sixty years vicar of this parish, and its traditions have been constantly kept up by a succession of noted Evangelical priests.

The Round Church

From Holy Trinity we pass down Sidney Street and into Bridge Street. Just opposite St John's Chapel is the church of the Holy Sepulchre, generally known as the Round Church. This is one of the four churches of the Templars which remain in England, and is the earliest. The Temple Church in London was built several years later; St Sepulchre's at Northampton is later again; and the round church at Little Maplestead in Essex belongs to quite the last years of the Order. The round portion of the Cambridge church belongs to the earliest Norman period, and was begun in the reign of William Rufus—that is, before 1100. It consists of eight divisions. The round-headed arches of the ground-floor rest upon massive round piers; dwarf piers on the same principle support the arches of the triforium, which include a double arch separated by a slender central pillar and springing from pilasters attached to the main piers. The clerestory above is lighted by eight round-headed openings, splayed inwardly. The ribs of the conical roof continue into the clerestory and triforium and finish in the spandrils of the triforium arches with grotesque corbels. Although all this is on a miniature scale, the effect is very grand and solemn. The good taste of the last century blocked up the triforium and filled the ground-floor with pews. The exterior had been adorned much earlier with an upper storey. This, to be in harmony with the late Perpendicular chancel, was crowned by an ugly battlement. In 1841, the Cambridge Camden Society took the church in hand. Their architect was Salvin, who restored it very well, taking down the upper storey, adding a conical slate roof in agreement with tradition, and opening out the Norman doorway. Unfortunately, the Society's taste in stained glass was not very advanced, and the gaudy east window by Willement is not at all appropriate. Wailes' glass in the round part is much better, but is not all that could be desired. The Society's stone altar was the subject of a *cause celèbre*, and was pronounced illegal by Sir Herbert Jenner Fust in 1845. This unhappy incident was the result of the dissolution of a society which had done literally everything for the cause of Cambridge archæology, and was no small factor in the great Church revival of the forties. St Sepulchre's is one of those rare livings which are in the gift of the parishioners; and the burgesses of the parish are very tenacious of their privilege.

Lower down, on the same side of Bridge Street, a very ignominious spire invites us to St Clement's, a church in the gift of Jesus College. This spire was built from a bequest of Cole, the well-known antiquary, early in the century, and above the west door is inscribed the punning motto, "Deum Cole." The body of the church is Early English. St Clement's is the last church on the east side of the river. St Giles', just beyond Magdalene, is a large modern church with an unfinished west end, but its history is not uninteresting. There is no doubt that the priory church of St Giles stood on this site, under the shadow of the castle. A Norman arch from the old church has been incorporated in the south aisle of the present building; and, across the street, the interesting little church of St Peter, whose detail is partially Norman, doubtless served as an extra chapel. However, as the importance of the house increased, it removed to the suburb of Barnwell. We know that the monastery was founded by Hugolina Picot and her husband, somewhere about 1090. The Barnwell removal took place in 1122, under the auspices of Pain Peverel, standard-bearer to Robert of Normandy. In Barnwell, the squalid suburb of Cambridge which lies between the Newmarket Road and Parker's Piece, no remains of the actual priory exist. It stood somewhere near the ugly modern church, which, although it is the parish church of St Andrew the Less, is called Christ Church. The little Early English building further down the Newmarket Road was, we may presume, a parochial chapel served by the Benedictines of the priory. It now bears the proud but doubly erroneous title of the Abbey Church. And the beautiful Norman chapel at Stourbridge, close to the modern Barnwell Junction, stood in a similar relation to what must have been one of the principal of the lesser Benedictine houses in England.

However, no one, unless he is a philanthropist or an impressionist painter, will go out of his way to visit Barnwell; and very few casual visitors get as far as St Giles', unless they lose their way. The church of St Luke at New Chesterton, not far beyond, is a good modern building, and its spire forms a prominent feature in the view of Cambridge from the Ely Road. Returning to the Round Church, where the two main arteries of Cambridge meet, we turn to the right past St John's Chapel and the Divinity Schools.[9] Between the latter building and Whewell's Court of Trinity is a triangular space which is the site of All Saints' Church. All Saints' formed, rather more than thirty years ago, a somewhat interesting feature in the streets of Cambridge, for its tower projected into the street, and the pavement ran through an archway beneath it. It was removed when Whewell's Court was built, and Mr G. F. Bodley erected a handsome new church just opposite Jesus College. All Saints' is, like St Clement's, a Jesus living. This later building is the best of modern Cambridge churches. Its spire is very good, and the east window is a curious experiment by the late Sir Edward Burne-Jones and Mr William Morris. The present Dean of Lichfield, who is a Jesus man, has also enriched the church with a charming little window by Mr Kempe. However, old All Saints' has gone the way of one or two other Cambridge churches—as, for instance, the older St Peter's, which was taken down to make way for Little St Mary's, and St John the Baptist's, which was near Clare. This open space and disused churchyard are its only memorial. The column in the centre was the gift of one Mr Boott, an American, who wished to erect some memorial to Kirke White in Cambridge.

Before we return to Great St Mary's, we pass the Decorated church of St Michael, which was built by Hervé de Staunton in 1337, and served as a chapel to his foundation of Michael House. It is a fine church, a good deal modernised, but containing sedilia in the chancel, which are not unlike those at St Edward's. The stalls in the choir are very complete, and are very excellent examples of fifteenth-century woodwork. At the end of the south aisle is a picture of Charles I. which bears a very close resemblance to the famous frontispiece of the *Eikon Basilike*. When Henry VIII. amalgamated the numerous foundations in this quarter of the town, and founded Trinity College, this church, like Great St Mary's, became college property, and the living is still in the gift of Trinity. In St Michael's was buried Paul Fagius, the Lutheran Hebraist, who lectured in Cambridge and died there during the reign of Edward VI. His bones, however, were exhumed to gratify Queen Mary's Commissioners in 1557, and were burned with those of Bucer in

[9] These Schools were designed by the late Mr J. L. Pearson, R.A.

the Market Place. This is one of the few historical facts which we can connect with Cambridge churches. They are, architecturally speaking, much more interesting than the churches of many old towns, and people who are weary of the sameness of the churches crowded together in places like Norwich or Colchester will turn to these with relief. But their records are barren, and, although we know a certain amount about Barnwell Priory, we should like to know more. While of the Templars' church absolutely no record remains, and the building merely informs us with a baffling reticence that Cambridge must at one time, among its religious houses, have numbered a rich and important Commandery of that glorious but unfortunate Order.

INDEX

D

E

F

G

H

I

J

K

L

M

Q

R

S

T

V

W

Lector House believes that a society develops through a two-fold approach of continuous learning and adaptation, which is derived from the study of classic literary works spread across the historic timeline of literature records. Therefore, we aim at reviving, repairing and redeveloping all those inaccessible or damaged but historically as well as culturally important literature across subjects so that the future generations may have an opportunity to study and learn from past works to embark upon a journey of creating a better future.

This book is a result of an effort made by Lector House towards making a contribution to the preservation and repair of original ancient works which might hold historical significance to the approach of continuous learning across subjects.

HAPPY READING & LEARNING!

LECTOR HOUSE

LECTOR HOUSE LLP

E-MAIL: info@lectorhouse.com

9 789356 145856

Printed by Libri Plureos GmbH in Hamburg,
Germany

9 789356 145856